Praise for

WHY DOES DADDY ALWAYS LOOK SO SAD?

"A powerful book for any parent/father trying to understand their child's struggles living with ASD. The book sends an inspiring message that loving your child conquers challenges, and that parenting is about the journey in discovering each other!"

—**Maisie Soetantyo, M.Ed.**,
RDI® Program Certified Consultant,
Clinic Director, and co-founder of the CATCH clinic

"Jude Morrow's eye-opening personal story of being a parent with autism is inspiring. It sheds light on the unique challenges experienced by a father on the spectrum, and explores what happens when a kid with autism grows up!"

—**Harold "Hackie" Reitman, M.D.**,
founder of DifferentBrains.org

"In his remarkable first book, Jude Morrow takes us on a unique journey through the trials and triumphs of being both autistic and a single parent. Jude tells us about his childhood as an autistic person with all the challenges that presents and how becoming a social worker and helping others has strengthened him. Beyond that, this book, for the first time, shines a light on a rarely discussed subject: being an autistic adult. I applaud this book and recommend it to everyone. A stunning and original contribution to the broadening field of autism studies."

—**Ian Hale, PhD**, author, speaker, and autism expert

WHY DOES DADDY ALWAYS LOOK SO SAD?

A MEMOIR

WHY DOES DADDY ALWAYS LOOK SO SAD?

A MEMOIR

JUDE MORROW

Foreword by Bernie Siegel, MD
author of *365 Prescriptions For The Soul* and *A Book of Miracles*

BEYOND WORDS
Hillsboro, Oregon

BEYOND WORDS

8427 N.E. Cornell Road, Suite 500
Hillsboro, Oregon 97124-9808
503-531-8700 / 503-531-8773 fax
www.beyondword.com

First Beyond Words paperback edition April 2020
Previously published in 2019 in the United Kingdom under ISBN: 978-1-09-636928-8

BEYOND WORDS PUBLISHING is an imprint of Simon & Schuster, Inc., and the Beyond Words logo is
a registered trademark of Beyond Words Publishing, Inc.

For information about special discounts for bulk purchases, please contact Beyond Words Special Sales
at 503-531-8700 or specialsales@beyondword.com.

Managing editor: Lindsay S. Easterbrooks-Brown
Proofreader: Ashley Van Winkle
Design: Devon Smith
Composition: William H. Brunson Typography Services

Manufactured in the United States of America

10 9 8 7 6 5 4 3 2 1

Library of Congress Control Number: 2019954931

ISBN 978-1-58270-757-0
ISBN 978-1-58270-758-7 (ebook)

The corporate mission of Beyond Words Publishing, Inc.: Inspire to Integrity

FOR ETHAN

FOREWORD

Jude Morrow's book shares a lesson I learned years ago while working with cancer patients: There is always hope. All of us—as parents or children—need to accept that simple statement. When you do learn, desire and intention alter the world and cause things to happen that would not normally occur; and our mind and body become a unit instead of separate entities.

One of the biggest factors in a child's life is whether he or she feels loved or not by their parents. Those who do feel love live longer healthier lives. Parenting is really the most significant health issue there is. Just think about the fact that children become grandchildren to their parent's parents. Not a coincidence how grandparents judge you versus parents. I recommend we all become chosen mothers and fathers and love the children who choose us. We will save lives by doing that.

Jude makes a powerful statement: "Defeat makes a champion." I have run several marathons and once on the streets of New York a woman stood saying, "You're all winners!" over and over again. She was right because when you finish the race of life (or marathon in this case) you will receive your medal and know you made a difference.

Jude Morrow's book is his "journal of life" and I recommend we all write a "book" by keeping a journal of our life's experiences because by bringing forth what is within you, you truly save your life. I can also tell you that rereading your words years later is very therapeutic, so learn from Jude and start the healing process now.

When you live in your heart, magic happens. Read Jude Morrow's story and learn from his experience and make your life easier through his experience and wisdom.

—Bernie Siegel, MD,
author of *365 Prescriptions For The Soul*
and *A Book of Miracles*

PREFACE

The parenting journey is difficult for any first-time parent. With Asperger's, this brought new challenges: learning to interpret non-verbal cues, living my life according to my baby, and having to let go of my previous coping mechanisms to learn new ones. Ethan's earliest years were full of tears, tantrums, teething problems, sleepless nights, and confusion. Although I have to admit, 99.9 percent of these were from me and not Ethan.

I relied heavily upon my parents to help me build a positive relationship with Ethan and I certainly couldn't have managed without them. I had to go on an entirely different journey to get to where I am now.

I knew that Jupiter has seventy-nine known moons and where the swimming pool was located on the *Titanic*, yet I didn't know how to connect with this beautiful child who called me "Daddy." (For anyone interested, the *Titanic* swimming pool was on F-Deck above boiler room six.)

Trying to forge a connection when I can be naturally distant was exhausting for me, but the fact that Ethan could see my vulnerability in full meant that I had to change. One day I won! I will never free myself of Asperger's but I can learn to adapt to new situations, and this helped me connect with my son in a way I didn't think I was capable of.

When speaking of autism, I deliberately refrain from using the word "disorder." My reason for this is that I view autism as a gift to be celebrated and cherished, not a burden to be pitied.

I want to demonstrate that those with autism can be successful, be happy, and be good parents. I hope people can take comfort from reading about the journey I have been on, and thank you for bringing me on yours.

CHAPTER 1

My earliest memory of my quirky behavior is lining up my toy cars on the windowsill in our living room when I was just three years old. I would ensure that all the little door handles were perfectly aligned, facing the same direction on the windowsill overlooking Derry. I remember my mum wanting to dust the windowsill and the look of anguish when she wanted to dust at the expense of moving my toy cars.

We lived in a small apartment in the heart of the city's Bogside. Our home was quite odd in that it was a three-bedroom house although it was on top of another house. It was almost a hybrid between a second-floor apartment and a house. We had a huge living room window that had a spectacular view of the city and I loved to stare out of it and watch the world go by; I think we all did. I loved living there because there was carpet throughout the house (except for the kitchen and bathroom). I love the feeling of carpet on my feet and after we left this house in later years, Mum opted for wooden floors and tiles.

I was above average height and weight for a three-year-old. I looked older than my sister, Emily, who is two years my senior. Mum and Dad married and had children very young. They were both the youngest of their large families and wanted to grow up with their children. Mum grew up in the area we lived in at the time and her parents lived on the next street. My grandfather was eleven years my grandmother's senior and he passed away when I was very young. My dad's parents adopted him when he was a baby. They adopted him quite late in life and my memory of his parents is quite limited and he was raised in part by his much older siblings. His parents developed complex care needs in my early childhood and both passed away in nursing care when I was eleven.

Dad was working as accounts clerk and wasn't at home often during the day, leaving Mum to fend for herself against my quirky yet frustrating behaviors. Mum knew that moving my cars was the end of her day. One slight move of even one car was apocalyptic in my little mind. It was the end of the world. I couldn't verbalize very well and this resulted in many hours of screaming and hitting.

Despite this, Mum's warmth toward me is the same now at twenty-eight years of age as it was when I was three. When I come to visit her I get the same welcoming smile as I always did when she picked me up from playgroups or school. Mum and Dad were always proud of me and have stuck by me and defended me in almost every situation. I knew they were proud of me always, despite my social limitations that have always existed.

I went to two playgroups before I went to primary school. The first was a giant hall near where I lived. It was a huge open space that once operated as a nightclub. It had a high ceiling, a smooth lacquered floor, and not too many bright colors. I really enjoyed this playgroup and they had a box of toy cars for me to play with. Cars were my world and although my vocabulary and verbal skills were minimal, I could name any type of car passing the building. I was a little encyclopedia of contemporary and historic cars. So much so that the few words I could say clearly were car manufacturers.

This playgroup was like a haven for me. I had a whole new box of cars to organize on a step that used to be the stage in its former glory as a nightclub. I forgot that there were other children there. When someone approached me to play with the cars it was a different story. There would be a standoff between the other children and me for the cars. I wouldn't hand them over. Due to my size, I generated somewhat of a fear factor, especially with the staff. I was unpredictable and my wrath was something to be feared.

There was a chart of all the toys that were in the room along with our names. It would show the parents what their little treasures got up to in the playgroup. There was a sandbox, a water tray, paint, blocks, crayons, and of course my cars. I only ever played with the cars and nothing else.

The situation came to a head when children kept trying to play with the cars with me. I wouldn't allow this. In my mind the building would collapse if another child dared to play with the cars. One of the staff approached me, told me to hand over the cars and to share. I had no real concept of sharing because in my eyes I was performing a vital function within the playgroup. Nobody could organize those cars, only me. The staff member took the cars from me and I went berserk! I began to scream, punch, scratch, and cry in full view of the playroom.

I was back to square one. Back at home. Mum was told that the playgroup couldn't meet my needs and that I would have to go to one that catered for children with mixed abilities. Even at the age of three I could read and write. I couldn't communicate verbally but could understand everything those around me were saying. I have this image of myself staring out the window at the rain, knowing my cars were still in the playgroup that I couldn't return to.

My maternal grandmother was very present throughout my life. She was my mum's main support in the daunting task of helping me transition from childhood to adulthood. There were many occasions Emily and I stayed with her to allow my mum and dad to have some much-needed rest. I awakened around 4 AM every morning and would demand Mum come downstairs with me to play with my cars. Despite her tired eyes, she put on her large round glasses, her warm smile, and watched me play with my cars. It must have been agony for her waking at that time every morning and staying with me until very late at night.

When my son was born in 2013, I couldn't imagine not having my parents around to assist and offer me advice. Autism and Asperger's didn't have labels as we know them today when my paternal grandparents were growing up. The institutional care model of wartime UK and Ireland likely would have resulted in full-time institutional care had I been born in the 1930s. Children of differing abilities were viewed as the product of previous sin and wrongdoing in the eyes of the churches. I am glad I was born when I was.

Mum never gave up on me. She took me to some mother and toddler groups and I used to bring my cars from the windowsill with me. They were like comfort blankets for me and I felt complete with them, in the same way a crown completes a king. When I got down to my vital function of car arranging at one mother and toddler meeting, another parent approached Mum and asked her if I had autism. This wasn't something that she had considered before and I imagine there was a sense of denial. I would hate to think that before this lady approached her, she felt my behaviors were a result of being a bad mother or inadequate caregiver. I don't remember Mum ever shouting at me as a child or witholding affection toward me.

Writing about these times gives me a newfound respect for Mum and Dad that I never had. I almost feel apologetic for being the way I was. I could have been the blue-eyed boy. Instead I was aggressive, regimented, and my verbal skills mostly involved screaming and crying. I was a frightened child and prone to tears. I would lie in bed clutching my cars since I didn't trust anyone downstairs not to touch them while

I slept. Siblings can often play pranks on one another, although Emily never dared steal my cars, as she knew the tsunami of unimaginable terror that would befall her and the rest of the family if she did.

Mum started her own quest to take me to specialists. She wanted to find out if I had autism or other forms of learning disability. It was clear that I functioned higher than the average three-year-old, although only intellectually. I could read, understand prompt cards, and follow the instruction. My biggest setback was that I still couldn't speak. I went to medical appointments knowing that I was to be taken away from the routine of arranging my cars at home. On several occasions, I destroyed the waiting room to the point where Mum and Dad had to admit defeat and take me home.

I was taken to see a geneticist to find if there was a genetic cause for my yet-undiagnosed condition. Before she could tell what little she had to tell, I kicked her in the shin and ripped her blouse off. Mum and Dad laugh about this now but I imagine this was quite embarrassing for them at the time. I have to admit I find this slightly amusing as well.

Following many battles with pediatric teams and many casualties along the way, I was referred to a new playgroup that catered for children with mixed abilities and differing needs. The new playgroup was very different visually. It was attached to a local health center and care home for the elderly. It was a small and unassuming red brick building on the outside. Inside, the playroom bloomed to life as soon as I entered. There were so many bright colors and pictures on the walls. I immediately felt more comfortable as it gave a sense of order the previous playgroup didn't have. It was much more welcoming. The difference in my eyes was going from a dark and dreary hall to the penthouse suite in the Ritz Hotel, Paris. I have never stayed there although I hear it is lovely!

It didn't seem as chaotic to me and was more organized. The previous playgroup had a collective white noise that frightened me, but the new one sounded as sweet as a metronome. I remember the staff-to-child ratio was much higher, too. There were more opportunities for individual work with the staff and I enjoyed the one-on-one attention. I was used to singular attention at home, although Emily was very much present. She must have understood in her early years that I was a much more complex character than she was.

In this new playgroup, I could play with the cars without distraction and even allowed some of the other children to join—though I was always very much in charge. I didn't feel as different in this environment because some of the other children were like me. They had their own jobs to do and I had mine. Other children could be arranging paintbrushes or counting the floor tiles. We all knew our roles within the group and it was much more structured. We were all experts in our given fields and trusted one another greatly. Due to this, the playgroup ran like clockwork. Almost like a factory assembly line.

In this playgroup I met a new friend. His name was Ben and he had Down syndrome. I allowed him to play with the cars with me and enjoyed his company. We became very close. He wasn't as mobile and had difficulties with walking and movement. Mum informs me that I was very kind and protective of Ben. One Christmas, Santa came to visit our playgroup and parents were invited to come along. Ben took his place on Santa's knee and we were all taking turns to tell him what we wanted for Christmas.

Ben was so enamored by Santa that he wouldn't get off his knee. Mum began to panic as it was approaching my turn to sit on Santa's knee. Ben had behavioral needs very similar to mine and was territorial. As I approached Santa, Mum's heart rate increased, as Ben was in danger if he didn't remove himself from Santa's knee by the time it was my turn. But, that day I allowed Ben to remain with Santa. It was at that moment I displayed some form of empathy and compassion for another human being. I think Mum realized at this point that perhaps I wasn't so bad! It's nice to know that I allowed this at such a young age.

The playgroup staff was so kind, not just because there were a lot more of them. They were obviously trained and educated on the nature of our conditions. I felt really involved and remember drawing and painting pictures. I remember copying down words from signs onto the paper I had in front of me. The room was very colorful and had signs and pictures to describe what certain objects were. It must have been strange for the staff looking at the group's pictures: drawings of Mummy and Daddy, houses, and then my page, which had "ENSURE DOOR IS CLOSED AT ALL TIMES—THANK YOU."

I remained at the playgroup until June of 1995. I vaguely remember Mum and Dad telling me that I wouldn't be going back and that I would be going somewhere else in September. This was primary 1. I had a false sense of security of school because I thought it would be like the playgroup I was in. I arrived at the playgroup in the morning, did my duty to the best of my ability, and went home. But it was clear that I didn't have a learning disability or a cognitive deficit, so I was assessed as being able to go to a mainstream school. Sadly, some of my little comrades from playgroup did not meet the developmental milestones for mainstream education and went to different schools that could meet their needs.

September came quickly and I remember walking into this giant building—well at least it seemed giant to me at that time. I was going from one playgroup room to an entire school. The school was similar to my playgroup in that it was a short walk from my house, albeit in a different direction. It was an old building and had stood for at least a hundred years before I attended. I remember feeling excited. I had a uniform and felt that I would fit in somewhat if we all dressed the same, at least in appearance.

The classroom was compact, bright, and had displays of artwork on the walls. There were plants on the windowsill that would eventually bloom into sunflowers later in the school year. The classroom had small red chairs and four rows of desks for us all to sit at. In playgroup it wasn't like this and I wasn't the type to sit on a chair all day. I preferred to stand and couldn't verbalize this so I kept getting out of the chair. The teacher couldn't get me to stay put for any more than five minutes at a time. In my view the classroom was the Jude Morrow show; those who know me will probably mutter that not much has changed.

My primary school teacher knew a lot about me before I started in her class. I needed more support and she was only too happy to provide it. She knew I could read and by primary 1 I had a reading age of a ten- or eleven-year-old. I was able to write much more quickly than anyone else and I remember grabbing pencils and crayons from my classmates to ensure that their letters were written correctly. This was somewhat disruptive and my teacher gave me books to read to distract me from my illiterate peers. More often than not, I would have the book finished before I got back to my seat.

My struggles became apparent very quickly. Break times were the worst time for me. The playground was much too chaotic for me. In every direction different activities were taking place; some were playing football, some playing hopscotch, and other games. Amidst the noise and chaos of the playground warzone I stood quietly beside my teacher. I never remember her encouraging me to go and play and we developed an understanding that lasted for the entire school year.

My last playgroup was much more structured and I knew what to expect every day. In primary school, there was a lot more variety and I couldn't identify a clear structure like I had learned to do previously. I was able to read, write, and comprehend but I just couldn't bring myself to join in play with this group at all. I imagine it was very frustrating for my teacher. She met with my parents and explained everything. I can't imagine how defeated and sad Mum and Dad were when they were told that I didn't speak to anybody and frightened the other children.

It was decided by the school that I should have an assessment for a special needs school. An assessor working on behalf of the school was to observe me in the classroom for a number of days to find if my needs could be met in their school. At the time I felt this was an extra support to me and that I could communicate with this person quite well. I remember so vividly what she looked like; she wore large glasses, had very long red hair, and seemed quite young.

After what seemed to be a few minutes, she stood up and left the classroom. I probably thought that I had done something wrong, or had upset her in some way like I seemed to do with everyone else. It turns out she was disgusted at the thought that I was being considered for a school for special needs given my academic ability. It was suggested at the time that all my needs were behavioral and that I may not have had any form of autism at all. Instead of transferring to a school for special needs, it was recommended on her report that I would be assigned a classroom assistant to receive additional support in the class I was already in.

I would be allocated my own classroom assistant and she would accompany me for some class time and some individual work outside of the classroom environment. In 1995 most schools only had one teacher or assistant who would aid children with the additional needs and this school was no different. My parents were understandably relieved and quite happy with the outcome. Their little warrior had won again! There was also support and guidance offered to my parents to ensure that there weren't too many drastic changes between school and home.

The school was advised to play to my strengths, reading and writing. I learned to read at an alarming rate and the more I read the more I began to speak. At home Mum and Dad would read with me. I used to bring home several books at a time from school and they would both sit at the kitchen table with me as we read them together. They'd give me rewards for learning new words and phrases. I would nod to confirm that I understood what was being read to me. As my verbal skills developed I had issues with finding words. I found expressing myself difficult and I was frustrated. It took practice. I remember learning how to speak with Mum and feeling like I was letting her down. I knew the alphabet and the written word but couldn't get words out appropriately. Mum and Dad must have spent hours working with me at the expense of my sister's schooling. My speech was improving leaps and bounds although I had issues with sequencing and processing information, especially if there was too much.

Trying to communicate verbally was so difficult. Even as an adult I notice that I can have difficulties finding the right words, or I'll just stop dead in the middle of talking. The only way I can describe it is this feeling of being on holiday and wondering if the door is locked. I felt like this all the time—if a teacher or a classmate tried to speak with me, I felt the dread of not getting the right words out to them. I communicated through touch, both affectionately and aggressively. Not being able to speak fully made me overly affectionate and physically aggressive in equal measure.

I was referred to a speech therapist to aid my slow, clunky, and erratic speech. The speech therapy sessions didn't happen in school, but were held at a local health center. I was glad to get out of school for a short while periodically and I remember playing with toy frogs that jumped after I had pressed them. I was so preoccupied with these toy frogs that I was unconsciously learning to speak. The therapist covertly teaching me to speak was a linguistic ninja!

Learning to speak was exhausting. I was eventually able to release my words, but my use of language wasn't always appropriate to the context of the conversation I was trying to take part in. My passion for reading wasn't diminished with my newfound ability of speech. Instead I practiced talking by reading aloud from the books I loved so much, but I still couldn't use my words to converse with others. The more I began to speak, the more I felt I was able to join in with the rest of my class, but it was still difficult. I imagine the joy of being able to communicate with my classmates probably made me more approachable and easy to be around.

I started to take part in games. I enjoyed playing football but I could become overly excited, aggressive, and had to withdraw from the game if I gave away possession or tried too vigorously to regain it. I joined in with different groups without specifically belonging to a particular one. I can remember the vast majority of my classmates: their names, appearance, and how they were around me. Some were very friendly and understanding although others were understandably more sheltered and frightened. I was very tall for my age, even at five years old, and have now grown to be six feet four inches as an adult.

My struggles in school continued. For my parents, it seemed the overcoming of one obstacle led to being immediately confronted with another. When I learned to speak, I just wanted to talk and sing to everyone. This made me a target for bullies. I would become irate if I felt I was being criticized or belittled and I reacted aggressively toward them. On the playground and in the classroom, I was often told to stand away from the class during a particular activity. To me, this wasn't much of a punishment, as I hated sitting on a chair for too long, anyhow.

Mum was taking part in an adult training program at the time and she was placed in my school as a classroom assistant. Sometimes I playfully doubt this story. Perhaps she was coming into the school to gather intelligence on how I was during the day, quietly satisfied that I was as difficult in school as I was at home.

I don't remember actually clinging to Mum or seeking her out during the school day although I remember her being on the playground. I was too busy trying to fit in to care too much as to what she was doing. I was allocated a classroom assistant of my own who would sit with me during my classes. She was an older lady who had a lot of time for me. She would approach and speak to me on the playground when nobody else would. She encouraged me to speak although I used gestures and wrote down what I wanted to say. My condition means that I can remember almost anything that I read without knowing the exact context, or even comprehending it.

She'd lay out cards in front of me with different facial expressions on them. She would ask me how I felt and I would point to the happy face, angry face, or sad face depending on how my morning had been. She was so kind and I always looked forward to seeing her. Our one-on-one work together gave me a sense of safety at school The main focus of her work with me was to use the words that I had learned to converse with my peers.

I remember looking at words and not being able to verbalize them; I knew what they were and what they sounded like, but I just couldn't exercise my vocal chords to say them. In adulthood I trained and qualified as a social worker. When I care for people with expressive dysphagia resulting from a stroke or dementia, I immediately feel a sense of empathy toward their pain of not being able to verbalize. The frustration of not being able to do anything immediately causes me to give up or become agitated. I have to admit that this behavior and attitude has remained in specific areas of my life. If something doesn't come naturally to me as an adult, I tend to be defeatist.

I was a vulnerable child and I remember the sadness in my classroom assistant's eyes. At this point, I had developed a single tone, which was more of a shout than a speaking tone. I clearly recall the encouraging look she'd adopt while teaching me appropriate responses to certain questions or focusing my tone of voice. She brought me a sense of calm during our individual work and I could feel myself progressing. Mum and Dad were much happier and they felt they could bond with me much better.

A prime example of where my communication skill level was at during this time was how I'd start a new conversation. I would immediately begin to talk about a book I was reading or how I was feeling to my classroom assistant without greeting her or asking how she was. She taught me how to start and maintain positive conversations with my peers. I spoke incessantly about things interesting to me to my apathetic peers. I had very narrow literary and playtime interests; I couldn't understand why other children didn't share and bond over my interests with me.

I continued to make progress and I was learning to detach from certain objects or toys. I still had urges but my classroom assistant was there to encourage me during school hours and my parents were there for when I returned home. I still played with my cars but every so often, I would reluctantly give my mum or dad one to play with. I took the lead in playtime but subconsciously I was learning to let others in and to share.

With Mum and Dad's support, as well as my classroom assistant, school was becoming much easier. I actually enjoyed going through the gates and even ventured into the unknown territory of making friends. Although these friendships were probably mostly based on their fear of me (remember I was much bigger than the average five-year-old), I saw and experienced them as my friends regardless. My speech was progressing quite well and I was becoming quite articulate and well-spoken, considering not long beforehand I had the same vocabulary level as a Chihuahua.

I had progressed so well throughout my first year of school that Mum and Dad's lives were much easier with me at home. They started to enjoy taking me places and I was fitting in much better with my peers at school. My parents bought a caravan at a site in Kerrykeel, County Donegal, and we spent most of our summers there. I don't remember any specific incidents during these summers. I imagine Mum and Dad were much more lenient given I had vast open spaces to expend my almost unlimited energy. In earlier years, Mum couldn't take me to the supermarket or into town often because if I had a meltdown it was in full view of the general public. I would kick, hit, scream, throw myself on the ground, and refuse to get up.

Triggers for my meltdowns would have been disorganized shelves in the supermarket or viewing something I perceived to be pretty in someone else's shopping cart. Even if someone had a brightly colored bottle of bleach in their cart, I was firmly of the belief that I was missing out and we too, had to have it. I quickly outgrew the child seat in the shopping cart and had to walk beside Mum. She couldn't restrict my movement in the same way the cart could, and I was quite agile, to the point Mum couldn't catch me if I had chosen to flee.

Although I had progressed positively, my quirks and ritualistic traits remained. I was able to show that I could adapt to specific environmental situations, such as school, and my classroom assistant showed me how to be kind to others and allow them to play alongside me. I got such a rush out of it. Things were certainly starting to look up for me. In mountaineering, climbing the mountain is half of the challenge; in my eyes I had summited Everest against all odds. I survived the first few years of mainstream school and was progressing quite well. Although nobody told me that whenever you scale the highest mountain, you have to face the real challenge of getting back to the ground alive.

CHAPTER 2

By primary 5, I was nine years old. Most of the physical aggression and tearful tantrums had stopped and I had the same vocabulary range as everyone else in my class. I remember enjoying going to school. By most accounts, I had learned to adapt to certain situations. Primary 5 was a big turning point for me as the teacher I had was a young man and I felt I identified with him better.

I remember him being very kind and soft-spoken; he would never raise his voice and was quite timid for his profession. He certainly didn't rule by fear nor did he intimidate me in any way. I was quite eager to impress and make a good first impression. He was full of praise and had his own custom-made stickers that he would place in my exercise books if I had done good work.

My ritualistic behavior still very much existed, and I would organize certain items in the classroom and my classmates found this frustrating. I would adjust everyone's coats on their coat hangers and was often told to stop. An incident occurred when I was organizing books on the shelves; one of my classmates was walking across the classroom when he tripped on one of the books. He crashed to the floor and I immediately ran to see if my book collection was well, not my stricken classmate. I was more concerned with my sense of order than the well-being of others, a theme that would continue into adulthood.

My new classroom was a lot duller. My earlier classrooms were full of bright colors and pictures, but this one was a lot more grown-up. It didn't appeal to my senses as much. There weren't any sunflowers blooming on the windowsill and it felt much more businesslike. I admit it was slightly intimidating: yet another change in environment for me to grow used to. Like every change I had in my life, it took time.

I was always a prolific reader and by this time nothing had changed. By October, I had read every book in the small wooden library at the back of the classroom. I read during class time and would often take two or three books home to read at night. My teacher often had to go to other classrooms to get more books for me to read. The class was divided into reading groups and they would all read the same books. One group would read *James and the Giant Peach*, while the other group might be reading *Matilda*, and then there was me with my own reading group, reading *Tales of the Unexpected*. It was the same author so I didn't feel too left out.

Playing to my strengths seemed to give me a sense of order and control within the classroom. I had a clear structure of what I was going to do and my teacher set time aside for me every day to discuss the different books I was reading. He once brought me a copy of R. M. Ballantyne's 1858 novel *The Coral Island: A Tale of the Pacific Ocean*. I loved the book so much that he allowed me to keep it. I used to read one chapter every night and tell him what had happened the following day. I loved talking about the shipwreck adventure and the juvenile heroes.

At nine years old I didn't manage change very well. I was so set in my routines and I felt that as soon as I was used to a classroom in previous years, it was time to move up to the next one. My classmates were enjoying their new classroom but I often would visit my previous classrooms just to have a look inside. I'd look at the new pupil sitting in my old chair, in my old room, and felt quite sad. I tend to grow attached to people and objects quite quickly and I couldn't let go of my previous classrooms or teachers very easily.

While I was able to communicate now, I still felt quite lonely during breaks and lunch times. I didn't fit in well with my classmates and I didn't really know what my role on the playground was. I know now that my classmates weren't marginalizing me intentionally, although that's the way I thought at the time.

I was constantly frustrating teachers and classmates with my ritualistic routines and often struggled when I felt the day wasn't going my way. In the school cafeteria I hated changes to the menu or if I had to sit in a different seat. Learning to adapt is something I now realize is an ongoing process for me. Through primary school, university, and becoming a parent, I have always had to adapt and remold my thinking as I evolved and progressed through life.

When adapting to one issue or situation, another always seems to appear in its place and become my next challenge. As I was verbalizing much more clearly at this point, I began to mix with my fellow classmates much more easily. I felt quite included at times, although there were others who saw me for the easy target that I was.

Controlling my emotions was always difficult. When I couldn't communicate how I felt, I resorted to hitting if I was angry and a hug if I was happy. My individual sessions with the classroom assistant continued. The new focus of the time we had together was to control my emotions, which were either on full display or entirely absent—not in the same sense of what I now know a person with bipolar disorder might display, but more with acting appropriately to any given situation.

The biggest example I have of this goes back to the warzone playground. I had by this stage made progress in navigating the playground. I was a keen footballer and given my size and strength, I played very well and was able to fit in with the other boys in my class when it came to the game. In earlier years everyone was a winner and it was the participation part that counted. By primary 5, playtime evolved to having winners and losers. I couldn't, and still can't, lose very well. Losing a game of football ruined my entire day and I wasn't able to channel the energy of defeat into inspiration for win the following day.

I allowed minor mishaps to evolve into bigger problems in my mind. If I was on the losing side in any playground game, my schoolwork suffered. I would spend many hours analyzing every part of the game and where everyone else went wrong as I was never at fault, ever. I always sought out someone to blame and this didn't really work for me too well. Eventually, I was told to stop playing football at break and lunch times. When I was sent back to the classroom, I often stared out the window, watching everyone have fun.

My weekly individual sessions with my classroom assistant continued. They were mostly in the mornings when I came into school, but if they were in the afternoon, an incident could have occurred that hampered my ability to participate fully. The memories of these sessions are much more vivid than the earlier sessions. By this stage, I hadn't actually been diagnosed formally with any specific condition, although my classmates and teachers must have known I was on the autism diagnostic criteria for sure.

In the late 1990s, theater and drama groups were becoming very popular for those with special educational needs and autism. It was a safe place to shout, stamp feet, and expel some of the energy within. I was encouraged by my teacher to audition and volunteer for roles in our school plays. My size, stature, and booming voice were ideal for some of these productions. One in particular was *The Wizard of Oz*. I desperately wanted to be the Lion although I couldn't sing. I was cast as the narrator because of my confident reading voice that had developed over the years. I needed a lot of encouragement from my teacher to build up the confidence of speaking in front of crowds and seeing him amongst the audience in rehearsals was a great comfort to me. With individual encouragement, I felt capable of facing my fears and forgetting my perceived shortcomings.

I brought my script home and I was able to memorize it very quickly. I did have it on hand during performance nights but seldom consulted it as I had read it that many times. Mum and Dad's faces in the audience are a vision I will never forget. Their son who couldn't speak was now showing off his confident speaking voice to an audience of at least one hundred parents and teachers. They were so proud.

Taking part in the school drama and theater group worked wonders for my confidence. The school's music teachers were happy to have me and I was even happier to be there. Working in a scripted and organized environment relieved the pressure of having to think on my feet and come up with appropriate responses to random questions and discussions that would come at me. I knew exactly what to expect and what I was going to say in return.

Looking back on it now, I know the school was attempting different educational approaches with me that are designed to meet the needs of autistic students. I certainly cannot criticize those, but being involved in drama was probably the biggest help to me. As a father, I would love my own son to have the structured environment and stimulation that this offers. As a child I thrived in this area, so much so that when I returned to class I would shout out any answers to questions, refusing to raise my hand as expected.

The best analogy for my struggles in primary school is Anton Chekov's short story of the oarsmen. The oarsmen are rowing in choppy waters. Despite rowing tirelessly they are making very little progress. As soon as I had cleared the wave of one issue, another appeared directly in front of me. I suppose I was glad to have my teacher, classroom assistant, and my parents in the boat rowing with me.

My parents maintain that primary 5 was the year that gave me the most improvement and the single happiest year of my schooling. I don't remember much of primary 6 although I knew it would be my last year at the school. My parents had purchased a new house on the other side of the city and leaving me in that school was too great of a challenge given their own working commitments. For primary 7 I would have to move to a different school.

I knew I was leaving my primary school and remember missing it and being disappointed that I wasn't going back. My primary 6 teacher encouraged me to make a card for my classroom assistant who had stood by me and nurtured me since I was only five years old. I took this task very seriously and I started from scratch numerous times before I ended up with a final product. I had been accepted into an integrated primary school on the other side of the city and by this stage Emily had already progressed to secondary school. I had one more session with my classroom assistant in which I gave the card. I remember clearly the message I had written inside: "Thank you, I will always be your friend."

The summer of 2001 was the last summer we had in our caravan in Donegal. Mum and Dad decided that it was too much of a financial burden on them and had to let it go. I remember being devastated at yet another change although I was too young to understand their financial situation. It was their wish to go on cheaper foreign holidays instead of staying on our own rain-soaked island.

I have always taken sensory comfort from certain things. In our old caravan, I loved the sound of the rain bouncing off the roof as I lay in bed. I loved staring out the huge Perspex window at the front of our caravan; we were in a good spot overlooking the bay. Sadly another thing I would have to leave behind.

I arrived at my new school and from the exterior, it was much different from the school I had come from. This school was very modern, barely ten years old. This was an integrated primary school that welcomed students of all religious and cultural backgrounds.

This classroom was different to other classrooms. It was the first classroom I had that included a computer. My behavior of clinging to certain things had never fully left me—despite the efforts of all the individual sessions I had—and I immediately won sole custody of the computer. I didn't encounter much opposition and my teacher understood that my use of the computer settled me and stopped me from interrupting the class.

I started primary 7 quite nervously. It was an entirely new class and I didn't know anyone, being the new kid. I assume my teacher was quite well briefed prior to my arrival, especially regarding my challenging behaviors that very much still existed. I was now brimming with confidence, almost bordering on arrogance. I never raised my hand to answer a question. If I knew the answer, I simply shouted it, and my teacher was quite frustrated with this.

My new school's approach to me was slightly different. I didn't have my own personal classroom assistant, but one was present for the entire class. I liked this arrangement somewhat because I didn't feel singled out in front of the rest of my class.

This was the year of the dreaded eleven-plus exam. My parents and teacher were unsure whether to put me through it or not. It caused considerable discussion because I was academically and intellectually capable of going to grammar school if given a chance, but my behavioral and psychological issues placed me in a vulnerable position, and I was unable to sit in an exam environment. At times I found the classroom overwhelming; if it was noisy I would put my hands over my ears and close my eyes.

I was able to complete the practice exams at home in my own surroundings; in the classroom it was a much different story. I found it much too difficult to concentrate and focus. Even if I was able to complete the exam in a more controlled environment at home, would I be able to do so in a crowded exam hall? It was a dilemma for the school. It wasn't normal at that time for someone to complete an exam on their own with their own examiner.

Behind the scenes, it had come to a stage where I would be able to participate in psychological tests to determine what my diagnosis should be. As I was in my final year of primary school, I needed a statement of educational needs to carry with me to secondary school. I had gone to different appointments with my mum over the years and she was always told I was too young to diagnose definitively. In most circumstances a diagnosis of a higher-functioning autistic is made in early adolescence.

After many discussions as to how I would go through the academic selection process, I was provided with a room of my own in the school, and an examiner was present. I certainly would not have had the attention span or emotional skills to endure the intense environment of the academic selection process. Doing the exam with my classmates present would surely have resulted in failure. I wanted the challenge of completing the exam, although I was told that the exam I would be taking would be slightly different to the test my classmates would be doing.

This test was very similar to the standard eleven-plus exam, although there were some slight differences. It was an intellect-based test to measure my IQ and academic ability. It was the same as my classmates in that I was measured on my numeracy, literacy, and scientific reasoning. I remember sitting for the exam and the quiet room allowing me to focus solely on the questions. The hour allocated to complete it seemed to go by in an instant and I forgot the examiner was even present. The reading passage in the exam, by the most peculiar coincidence, was from *The Coral Island*. I left the room feeling confident that I had done enough to pass. I was relieved when it was finished. Nobody seemed to mind or judge that I was allowed to complete the test on my own. I don't remember anyone passing comment.

When the results came home to me, I was delighted to hear that I had passed the academic criteria to go to grammar school. My parents were not as surprised, as they had always known that my academic ability was very good, but even with the great progress I had made, I was still quite vulnerable and my behavioral issues still continued. At this stage, my GP ruled out ADHD as the cause of my challenging behaviors, and my ritualistic behavior continued. I was able to focus on certain situations although tasks involving others were very complex to me.

After the selection test, our class took on a new, exciting project: to write, compose, and perform an opera. We had to write a full script, design our own costumes, and promote the show itself. I thrived on being the center of attention given my newfound confidence developed during my early ventures in drama at my last school, and so I was appointed to be the show's production manager. As the weeks progressed, my teacher realized that he had made a grave error.

We all had different roles and responsibilities and I enjoyed overseeing every department, ensuring everything was completed to my standards. I had a clear vision of what I wanted and I didn't wish to hear any suggestions from others. It often led to arguments and admonishments from my teacher. We had an external facilitator come to teach us different techniques of putting on a stage show. I refused to allow him to cause disruption to my show. He was only a renowned theater director, singer, songwriter, and winner of numerous accolades. What did he know? My attention to detail and perfection alienated me from the rest of the class, and indeed the facilitator as well.

While being production manager, I began to moonlight in other roles: as a sound engineer, costume designer, scriptwriter, songwriter, composer, motivational speaker, catering manager, roadie, makeup artist, advertising team leader, orchestra leader, lighting engineer, and overall company manager. I arranged multiple dress rehearsals and cast the show by myself. I didn't cast myself in the play as I couldn't stand at the back of the hall and direct. I let some of my classmates carry out menial jobs, although I normally changed what they had done after they left the area.

It was obvious that I wanted things done a certain way. I couldn't listen to any suggestions from my classmates and I completely disregarded how they felt about being excluded. I didn't demonstrate any empathy toward them nor did I want the show to deviate from what I wanted it to be. These behaviors were observed and noted by my teacher throughout the entire project. I spent hours drawing plans for the stage and even made several scale models of what I wanted the stage and backdrop to look like. Often these would take days and I could not be disturbed when making them. The whole thing became an obsession, although at eleven years old, I didn't realize this and believed all my contributions were both positive and necessary.

Given the production value of my masterpiece, I must have gone severely over budget. I would be surprised if the school's nursery had any money left to give the little children milk and fruit. When my masterpiece was completed, I felt the same sense of achievement Stanley Kubrick must have felt when he finished filming *Spartacus*. Obviously, my teacher had completely given up trying to stop me from hijacking the production many weeks previously.

By March my show was completed and ready to be publicized to the world. The tickets were designed by a group of girls who had also designed the costumes for the play. I later changed the ticket design and reprinted them before they went on sale. Our play was about a group of children stranded in school during a snowstorm. As the story was about school, I had pulled props from throughout the school for an authentic atmosphere. I was proud of the cast as I stood in the wings watching the show. Such was my arrogance that I joined the cast on stage for the curtain call at the end.

After the show we had a school trip to look forward to. We were told that we were going to an outdoor activity center in Donegal for a few days. We stayed in a large country house in the Donegal countryside beside a lake. I always enjoyed the outdoors and my dad had taught Emily and me to swim when we were younger. I ran before I could walk and I could swim before I could talk.

On our first day we were split into two teams. Our challenge was to build a raft for a race across the lake. We were all instructed to work as a team to design a raft that everyone could sail on together. Like my now-defunct opera company, I dismissed the rest of my team and decided to build the raft myself. I took this very seriously and believed that I could come up with a nautical marvel that would become the future of raft building. Needless to say the raft I built was a beauty! I had tied the provided barrels together for improved buoyancy and handling. Instead of having a sail I asked for a canoe paddle, so that I didn't have to depend on wind speed and direction to get where I wanted to go.

The staff happily humored me and provided me with a paddle so I wouldn't require a sail for my raft. As usual, I knew much more than they did and I told them that a sail was not appropriate for the raft I had designed and built. I made sure the opposing team knew that my raft was by far the better beast, and that I would have tea and sandwiches ready for them for when they eventually crossed the lake in second place.

I proudly brought my raft to the lake and refused to allow my team-mates on board. After some negotiations with my teacher, I allowed my teammates onto my raft. As we boarded the raft and waited for the whistle, I was disappointed. I wanted to command and pilot the raft to victory on my own. As the whistle rang out across the lake I paddled with unimaginable fury. My raft held strong and true . . . for a grand total of around twenty seconds.

As the ropes binding the barrels came loose, I blamed my entire sailing crew for what was happening. We were taking on water and the structure was becoming weaker. Instead of taking responsibility and inspiring my crew of doomed sailors, I dived into the water and swam back to the starting line. I watched the other raft sail effortlessly to the other side of the lake whilst my barrels, ropes, and teammates were scattered across the lake. I knew I shouldn't have let them on the raft.

Of course the aim of a raft-building race is the act of building the raft as a team and having everyone distribute their weight to safely sail to the other side. In my mind, I didn't think like this, and the main object of the exercise was to win and show everyone what I was capable of. By now, I knew I was drastically different from my classmates. I wanted to impress to make up for my own condition and the shortcomings that came with it. The desire to impress and aimlessly chasing perfection certainly caused me more harm than good.

The second night we completed a nighttime walk. For the walk we would be taken to the forest, blindfolded, and would need to lead one another by the hand through a series of obstacles. I knew this was taking place later in the evening and I was afraid of it the entire day. I didn't like the prospect of having my vision taken away and having to allow someone else to be in control of whether I made it through the forest or not.

Night fell and we all gathered at the forest entrance to start the activity. We got into pairs and formed an orderly line. The group leader taking us through the forest could see and would warn the pair at the front of any obstacles along the way such as trees or bumps on the path. In turn, they would tell the people behind them and so on. I had the blindfold placed over my eyes and I immediately started to panic. I tried to remember all the breathing techniques and calming methods I had been taught over the years if I was frightened. The pressure was immense.

With my eyes covered, the sound of the snapping twigs was deafening to me and I could feel the sweat on the palms of my hands. I couldn't help but feel my tears seeping through the blindfold and my breathing becoming shallower. I pressed on until I felt my legs lock, causing me to crash to the ground. I couldn't cope with the deprivation of a sense and it led to a meltdown in the middle of the forest. I didn't take any comfort in the fact that I would have been kept safe had I listened to the instructions from the pair in front of me.

As I was often an easy target for bullies, I was taught by my parents and teachers not to take anything people said to me at face value. Even as an adult I find sarcasm very difficult and have an automatic doubting reaction when people tell me things. That school year was the start of a very toxic symptom. I naturally became very distrusting and often disregarded what people told me. I became very proud and started to portray an outgoing persona to mask my feeling of being different.

As a basic survival instinct, I often worried what others thought of me and desperately wanted to hide that I was different. I naturally don't fit into social groups and wanted to be the outsider at the center of attention. This was the toxic persona I wore to hide the shame and denial that I wasn't quite like everyone else.

I discussed this school year with my teacher many years later; he described it as the most perplexing experience he had in teaching to that point. He was able to laugh and so was I, although it made me think about how others felt about my actions. It made me feel guilty that I may have ruined certain experiences for other children growing up. I hadn't wanted to accept that I was different and I had held a very negative view of myself.

As the end of the school year drew to a close, I was faced with one final challenge. Throughout the years my mum and dad fought to get to the bottom of my social abnormalities. Most medical professionals need evidence of prolonged and enduring symptoms like the ones I was facing. In other words, they needed to see if I would develop beyond the symptoms and by that stage I clearly hadn't. While I had progressed, a lot of my difficulties remained. I was still ritualistic, in that I would only complete certain tasks at a certain time of day. I still found mixing with other children incredibly difficult and I didn't like any form of change at all.

The aim of this test was to ascertain and pinpoint my condition, so that the secondary school I would eventually go to would be able to prepare the appropriate support for me. Interestingly, when I was gathering notes for this book, my parents were unaware that this was the exact reason this test was conducted. They actually believed that this was another component to the academic selection process. I was used to completing individual work away from the class and having annual meetings to discuss my progress, so I believed this to be the same.

I met the examiner and she explained the test to me. There would be two components that she would explain as the test progressed. The first part of the exam consisted of very long questions that I often had to ask her to repeat. I manage well with short, concise questions but multiple questions can leave me confused as to what part I should answer or discuss first, and this has always been the case.

The second part of the test was a series of pictures that I was to note particular observations about. I remember very vividly one of the pictures: it was a supermarket and I immediately noticed that the labels from a row of canned foods were missing. I later looked at the test as an adult and noted there was also a sad-looking baby in the picture sitting on the floor. As a child, I was unable to pick up on this immediately.

I also completed the Ishihara color test, the test to assess for color-blindness. It was immediately apparent that I wasn't color-blind; I passed the test with ease. Another component of the exam was to describe the feelings of those in the pictures. There were many pictures and I had to assign an emotion to them; I found this incredibly difficult.

The examiner also had reports from my doctor and numerous primary teachers. It was clear that my social abnormalities were enduring. Although I met physical and developmental milestones, some were still missing. It was obvious that I needed continued care and support for when I made the transition into secondary school. It must have been a very concerning time for my parents. Their excitable yet vulnerable child was edging ever closer to adulthood.

Given the information gathered over the years and the outcome of this test, I was formally diagnosed with Asperger's syndrome. Mum had always suspected this and certainly wasn't shocked when my diagnosis was confirmed. Mum told me recently that she didn't remember being told of this formally but it is clear in my 2002 medical records. By that stage, a diagnosis had to be finalized to ensure I got the correct educational support I so desperately needed.

Differing forms of autism require adjustments to be made to ensure a child's comfort and success in education; I was no different at this stage. The report would be compiled to form an official statement of educational needs that would remain with me until I finished my education altogether. I wasn't told of my diagnosis at this time, as I was much too young to understand and probably would not have appreciated the label. I wasn't prescribed any medications at this point. My verbal and physical aggression had stopped several years prior, although it reappeared during the early stages of my secondary education.

The school year finished in June with yet another change on the horizon. I remember relishing the challenge of starting secondary school and felt ready. I enjoyed the rest of my final year of primary school although I would imagine my classmates didn't enjoy it as much as I did. I turned twelve during the summer and we went on our first foreign holiday to Spain. The heat and humidity overcame Emily and me and we argued for the majority of the holiday, to Mum and Dad's despair. I think this holiday was a taster to what would follow as I entered my teenage years.

Chapter 3

I started secondary school in September 2002. Up to this point, my mum and dad fought valiantly to gain the best outcomes for me. From when I was asked to leave my first playgroup up until now, I was experiencing one victory after another. It demonstrates how fragile my early education was. I went from having an assessment for a special needs school to gaining a place at one of the most prestigious Catholic grammar schools in Europe.

My secondary school was much different in that it was a school for boys. We wore black uniforms and the school was greatly influenced by local clergy at the time. I had visited the school during the summer with Dad when making the decision as to what school I would go to. The majority of my primary school classmates went on to integrated secondary education while a small number of us went to different schools.

I recall two others from my primary school class going to the same school as me, although they weren't in my new class and I barely saw them. The school was vast and very impressive, with different rooms for different classes. I didn't really like the idea of moving around the school at different parts of the day. I was so used to being in the one room for the day that I was anxious about having to go from one room to the next.

I was used to little changes being subtly implemented, but being thrown into an enormous crowd of pupils in an enormous building caused me a great deal of panic. My classmates could sense that I was quite nervous and in their eyes, quite odd. There was a classroom assistant present in my classroom although her attention was mostly directed toward another pupil. He must have had much more complex needs than I because he didn't speak often and it was clear that he struggled academically.

Birds of a feather tend to flock together so I tried making a conscious effort to speak with him. I was much better at social interactions and I remember him shaking when I tried speaking with him. He must have had a much more debilitating condition that I wasn't aware of at the time. As I can have difficulty interpreting body language and facial expressions, I dismissed him as rude and didn't speak with him again. Our classroom assistant sat with him in all of our classes and as time progressed he became more and more absent. I don't think he made it past Christmas. I wonder how he is now. I hope he received the same support and therapies as I did and that he is well.

I definitely experienced some regression when I went to secondary school. If I felt threatened or cornered by other pupils, I started to resort to physical aggression again. This started in the second term of my first year and my parents were frequently called into the school. I was never suspended for being aggressive as they were aware of the nature of my condition. I was progressing well academically, although socially I wasn't. I had become an easy target and was often physically and verbally forceful toward my classmates both in the classroom and outside of it.

As I still loved reading, I flourished learning different languages. My French and Spanish teachers were very impressed that I could learn to read, write, and speak another language so effortlessly From my previous experience in school plays, I had the confidence to learn to speak in a different language. I continued to read prolifically and I enjoyed the higher standard of the books available. I couldn't participate much in physical education, as I still hadn't learned to cope with losing and working as part of a team.

I did demonstrate natural ability in sports. My size and stature gave me a significant advantage although opposing players could provoke me much too easily. A foolproof tactic to stop me performing well was to call me names quietly while I was in earshot. My PE teacher often showed me the red card or asked me to leave the playing field. My temperament was just too volatile and this ruled me out from representing the school on their sports teams. Looking back on it, I don't blame them. I wouldn't have allowed twelve-year-old me to play either.

It was agreed with my parents that I would have individual sessions with the special educational needs coordinator (SENCO) once per week. As I entered my teenage years the hormonal changes for me rendered my previous therapies obsolete. In primary school my therapies were mostly play based but I was now beyond that going into my thirteenth year. I was able to share with my classmates when appropriate although secondary education is more discussion based than play based. At my new individual sessions, I would speak generally about my week and the work I was doing.

While I am not color-blind, I found out that I had trouble recognizing patterns, shapes, and matching colors. I struggled with art and didn't have the patience for it. It led to numerous disagreements with my art teacher. As a class we were tasked to paint a copy of Van Gogh's depiction of sunflowers and mine was singled out for critique. I couldn't blend the brush strokes on the canvas nor could I match the colors correctly. When she asked about my use of patterns and colors, I was dumbstruck and couldn't answer. When some of my classmates started to snigger, I became verbally aggressive toward her and stormed out of the room. I know in hindsight that not every teacher would have known about my educational needs, but this was of no consolation to me at the time, because I wasn't aware of them either.

I couldn't open my mind to receive other points of view and this caused me to become isolated. I have always been scientifically minded and I felt my condition doesn't allow for—what I believe to be—a faith in a deity. I work best with the immediate evidence of what is in front of me; anything abstract or requiring hypotheses troubles me. For example, boys support their own favorite sports teams, but if somebody didn't share my passion for a certain team, they were wrong.

As I wasn't mixing well with the other boys in my class, one of my teachers suggested to my parents that I join different groups and activities outside of school. My dad knew the coordinator of a local cross-community group and recommended I join. My region was recovering from the wounds of a sectarian conflict that lasted from the late 1960s to the late 1990s. The group was based in Derry city center and open to all religious faiths and backgrounds. It was a large group and I was quite nervous about going. This group was designed to promote peace and reconciliation amongst young people to prevent a return to the violent past we endured.

I signed up when I was fourteen and this would prove to be the making of me. This wasn't a group specific for those with autism, although Mum had suggested some of those types of groups before (but of course I had refused.) It was determined that I functioned much too highly to avail of any specific autism support groups. I didn't want anyone to know that I was different and I started my attempts to hide who I really was; I was so desperate to fit in.

By this stage, I had constructed a confident and outgoing persona to mask my own self-bitterness at the fact I was so different from everyone else. At face value, nobody else in the group suspected I was any different and I memorized specific mannerisms that other people had and passed them off as my own. I would examine how my peers greeted one another and try to emulate it confidently. Like any other trickster, I gained the respect of whoever was willing to listen. I was starting to finally mix with my peers, until I was brought down to earth one fateful day—the school fire alarm was triggered one afternoon and the noise sent me into a panic. I stood still and raised my hands over my ears to shut out the noise. Hundreds of pupils filed past me to go to the fire assembly point outside and I just stood anxiously inside the school waiting for the alarm to end. I felt my legs wobble when I finally made my way outside; I forced myself to remove my hands from my ears to make sure nobody could see my internal struggle.

The new group I joined met once per week and I always looked forward to attending. Mum left me with the group for the first time and I felt like I immediately fitted in. Within a year, I became chairperson of their Youth Committee, a member of the club's management committee, and was awarded the group member of the year award. I felt so accomplished. I was allowed to work in my own way and was able to gain support from the other group members. I felt so normal.

Prior to joining, my behavior was unpredictable and I didn't fit well into my class. In my youth group, we all had a common cause and purpose, to have our voices heard. The group would facilitate training and classes that provided me with credit toward a university degree. I completed training courses on sexual abuse awareness, autism awareness, community relations, and first aid. These were topics I had a particular interest in because I was quite naive as a young child and teenager. I was able to learn in school, but I wanted to know more about the society I felt I wasn't part of.

I completed funding applications on behalf of the group and I proved to be quite successful at this task, which was good since youth groups in Ireland are heavily dependent on government funding and charitable donations. My success was due to the fact that I was a very articulate and literate fourteen-year-old and my letters always looked perfect, especially when applying for funding.

The coordinator of the group was happy to give me extra responsibilities. I felt so touched that someone trusted me to help carry out a vital function on behalf of the group. No amount of individual work in the past helped me as much as being given responsibility. I enjoy challenges and thrive off the feeling that others trust me. Formal committees allowed me to observe their demeanor and learn. As a committee meeting is structured by an agenda or terms of reference, I knew when it was my time to speak and had adequate time beforehand to prepare.

The skills I was learning at my youth group helped me to bond with my other classmates and school became much easier for me. I was receiving a formal education in school and a real "life" education in my youth group. This group opened my eyes to what other young people were like. I was on the fringes of society, but I was able to safely look inside without fear of judgment. I was selected to go on exchange trips, and in 2006 I went on an international exchange to Bulgaria. I loved learning of other cultures and their languages.

Over the next couple of years, I flourished and bloomed so much that I started to make friends, or at least I thought of them as friends. I turned sixteen in the summer of 2006 and with the challenge of mixing with my year group surmounted, I was faced with vulnerability yet again. I was hungry to fit in with others, and by others, I mean anyone! Like every parent's worst nightmare, I fell in with bad company. I started smoking, drinking, and experimenting with drugs.

As I was tall and looked much older than sixteen, I was able to drink in bars very easily. Mum and Dad clearly didn't know where I was in these times. The group of friends I had made were from unfortunate circumstances and likely didn't have the same loving and caring parents as I did. At the time I respected my new friends' free-spirited and carefree nature (lucky for my parents, this phase was reasonably short). Nightclubs were a huge challenge for me; flashing lights, fog machines, lasers, and loud music triggered sensory overload and agitation. I often sneaked away and went home. I was glad to feel part of something, although I was so annoyed with myself when I went home after realizing I couldn't handle it.

When I first experienced a nightclub, I felt the same as I did when I was five years old and joined a playgroup. So many people doing different things: the crowded bar on one side and a whole dance floor on the other. I just couldn't fit into the situation and it frightened me as much at sixteen as it did when I was five. I never spoke of this fear to anyone at the time. How could I?

I suppose my Asperger's came to the rescue. I found it difficult to manage the loud, optical experiences nightlife brought and my flight response triggered. I would worry a lot, even now. I always believe that those who do not worry become complacent and prone to error. Situations such as these would cause me to panic and I always left, with or without excuse. I just couldn't function in this environment at that time, thus ending my short-lived rebellion

Every school year showed positive academic progress, and at sixteen I sat the last of my compulsory school exams. I passed every test with flying colors and went back to school for the final two years. I gained the confidence and ability to sit in an examination hall and complete my exams like everyone else. For any readers outside of the UK and Ireland, sixth form, as it is known, is unlike the American high school in that it is not compulsory and we can leave school at sixteen. I decided to remain at school as I wanted to go to university.

So the once nonverbal, aggressive child with significant behavioral and sensory issues returned to fight another day! It was when I was seventeen that I started to realize and query my condition for myself. I asked my mum what the nature of my condition was and what it was called. I remember her actually telling me at this stage that I had Asperger's. I didn't participate in as much destructive behavior, and I set myself a goal to go to university. As I had spent many of my formative teen years as part of a youth group, I decided that I wanted to become a social worker. I had completed many training courses that I used to support my application.

Imagine that! The person in my class with the most social difficulties actually wanted to become a social worker. Of all the careers I could have chosen, the one most unsuited to my limitations is the course I decided I wanted to pursue. I still don't understand my logic in this regard, even though I have been doing the job for seven years now. When I discussed my preferred option with the careers advisor she validated my decision and encouraged me to pursue this as she saw that I was quite a capable leader and decision maker.

Those two years brought me a wealth of experiences. I was asked to become a group leader at my youth group, which I must say I am still indebted to for their kindness toward me. I relished this challenge and was very well supported by the other group leaders. They knew I wasn't like most others but that I was capable of learning from them. I applied for and worked in two summer camps in the summers of 2007 and 2008. I loved traveling and meeting new people. I got a kick out of it. The summer camp structure suited me and every day was the same. When other staff got bored of the routine, I very much enjoyed it. I learned to water ski, rock climb, and drive on the other side of the road.

My youth group and parents saved my life. I didn't belong anywhere until my youth group allowed me to be myself and used my quirky traits to their advantage. When I took on projects I threw my heart and soul into them and I didn't stop until I got the outcome that I wanted. I would encourage parents of all abilities to seek out groups for their children to attend. My therapies throughout school taught me specific skills that no doubt helped, although being in a youth group helped me to learn about people.

In June 2009, I was eighteen years old and had left secondary school behind. It only seemed a short while ago that I was lining my cars up on my windowsill and now it was time for me to buy my first car. In my vast collection of cars, I was particularly attached to Volkswagen Beetles and Rovers of any sort. Most eighteen-year-old boys buy cars with sporting pedigree in order to impress the fairer sex—not me. I bought a 1999 Rover 75 saloon. Royal blue with a mahogany dashboard and chrome door handles. I was head over heels in love. My peers believed this to be a ridiculous car for an eighteen-year-old, as did my parents and almost everyone who knew me. I used to love driving it despite the odd looks people would give.

Starsky and Hutch were associated with the Ford Gran Torino; I was associated with my Rover 75. I cleaned it and obsessed over it. I became so attached to it that I got upset if anyone ridiculed it. Everyone recognized me from a distance and I suppose I liked that. In my late teens I focused so much on standing out when in times gone by, I just wanted to fit in.

I was accepted on to the social work degree and started my university studies in September 2009. The classes were mostly mature students with much more life experience and with a clear female majority. When I met my classmates for the first time I had no idea where I was going to fit in this group. My first day at university was a change that I had looked forward to; I didn't feel overly anxious and was comforted in knowing that I would get used to it like every change that had come before.

I sat in the vast jungle of lecture halls amongst so many students, most of whom had so many different life and work experiences. I remember coming home from a lecture about benefits and welfare and thinking to myself that I was a fraud. I had no idea of what issues other people faced nor did I understand them when I was told. I couldn't identify with those facing adversity although I had faced many adversities myself. I was a nineteen-year-old boy who probably should never have been there. Of course I gained a place on the course like everyone else although I didn't have what I perceived to be the right skills to survive in the profession. I was a terribly awkward young man and I couldn't relate to people very well.

I found myself relatively alone again. I didn't really fall into any groups because of my young age. Some members of the class were in their mid- to late twenties, although the age gap still rendered me relatively ostracized in the class group. By this stage I was aware that I had Asperger's and disclosed this to my course tutor, who commended me for being open. It was the first time I had told someone about the condition I had. Only my closest family and best friends knew. I remember being relieved and I was given assurances that I would receive any support I needed.

Finally taking the first step to be open helped me greatly throughout my university studies. Given their own professional backgrounds, my instructors understood my condition and how it could affect me. I asked one of my teachers how I could help people if I found it hard to read social situations and people's feelings. This was not an easy question to get an answer for, although I did receive one of the most encouraging pieces of advice. I was told to reflect on my past and what advantages I could bring to someone's life if given the task of supporting them.

I went home with my pen and notepad and thought about my times in youth group. I have a high level of passion and desire to gain results and would work tirelessly to achieve them. If I set myself goals and targets, I invest vast portions of my soul into getting the outcome I want. I thought that this would be useful in advocating for those much more vulnerable than I. I started to view the course much more positively and knew that I could make a difference to people's lives if given the chance. I started to integrate well into the class and enjoyed going to my lectures.

It was the first time that I believed my condition could become an advantage! Emotional attachment is always something I have struggled with. Being from a logical school of thought, I can view a situation for how it is as opposed to emotional sentiment clouding my judgment. It allowed me to retain my natural ability to step back, assess, and decide what should be done.

I didn't tell anyone else in the class I had Asperger's. I was still ashamed of it then. The academic nature of the first year suited me, as I could remember the necessary information for my assignments and understood the content when I read it thoroughly. Given my young age, my teachers were very kind to me and I didn't display that I was completely out of my depth. I had overcome so many battles that failure wasn't an option. I had to pass the course and gain my degree. I believed that I had many critics, and I wanted to prove everyone wrong. Sadly, what I perceived to be critics then were people only trying to help me.

I was something of a ghost in my first year of my degree; I didn't form many friendships nor were there many group tasks that would force me to communicate with others. I came to my classes, absorbed the content, and left. Facts, figures, legislation, policy, and statistics were easily retained, although ethical dilemmas were an issue for me. A common ethical dilemma in social work would be the issue of capacity and consent, especially with older people or those with learning disabilities. The dilemma being wishes verbalized by people with a doubt as to whether they have the mental capacity to understand their requests fully. A prime example would be an older person with dementia with no family, expressing their wish to remain at home when they have a long history of falls and forgetting to take medications.

Dilemmas presented gray areas for me and I could only see in black and white. I sided with one perspective that in my view was best, without regard to other factors. Weighing information and risk was a skill I hadn't learned, and I found this extremely challenging. I met with my tutor on an individual basis and explained my struggles with this—it often led to tears. I felt as if I was almost subhuman or even inhumane since I couldn't feel the pain of someone else. It took me a long time to realize that life isn't about feeling the pain of others but understanding the pain they are going through and why.

I did enjoy the student lifestyle and my parents were happy that I was mixing with others. I took my studies quite seriously and wanted to progress. I thrived off challenge and responsibility, and I liked learning about the society that attempted to ostracize me because of my limitations. I learned of the responsibilities I would face upon completion of the course and I wanted to prove that I could be a responsible adult in a professional position.

The second and third years of my studies were much more challenging. I had two six-month placements in both a childcare setting and an adult care setting. As I was only nineteen years old during my first placement, I didn't know anything about children or parenting. As I was quite young, I certainly lacked the life experience for the placement I was in, although the team supported me as best they could. Interacting with real people and real situations was quite troubling for me at first. At this time, I struggled to imagine myself as a parent. I never thought that in a few short years I would be a father myself. I didn't feel that I bonded properly with any of the kids I worked with, as I was so task-focused rather than intent on building relationships with them. I was so nervous that I found myself losing my speech again. I would be extremely nervous and my team knew this. We had days at the university to discuss our progress and I often lied about how well I was progressing. I felt it wrong to show weakness, although I'm sure my classmates would have been supportive. I just wanted to feel like everyone else, but I viewed everyone as progressing much further than I was.

Despite the challenge, I got through it with the support of my parents and classmates and progressed to the final year of my course in 2012. I was placed in a hospital setting and loved every second of it. I enjoyed the structure and clockwork nature of the acute care sector and I was able to play a positive role in the team for the duration of my placement. I loved learning about other professions and how everyone would come together as a team to achieve positive outcomes for vulnerable people. I didn't tell anyone in my new team of my condition, not because I was embarrassed, but rather for the first time, I didn't feel the need to tell them.

I remember eagerly logging in to the online student portal to find if I had passed my course. My placement had finished and all my final assignments were submitted. I remember reading my results and collapsing to the floor in my parent's house. I did it! I couldn't believe it and neither could they. I graduated on July 9, 2012—I was a fully qualified social worker. I walked across the stage with pride when I collected my degree; I couldn't believe it. My dad later told me that this was one of the happiest days of his life.

It proved that through strict perseverance, confiding in people, and setting myself a goal, I was capable of achieving anything. I was so proud of myself that I didn't have any fear in proudly walking across the stage in front of my peers to receive my degree. Keeping my composure was so difficult. As an adult I realized that containing positive emotions was almost as difficult as containing negative ones. If I didn't breathe regularly on the day of my graduation, I would have cartwheeled across the stage, sang a few songs, and given an inspiring speech on the topic of overcoming adversity. Sadly, other people were behind me and had to receive their degree.

I registered with a recruitment agency and began my career. I worked in an early-years team as an inspector for child minders and child day-care units. It was based seventy miles from home, although the fact I had worked so hard to gain my qualification rendered me indifferent toward the distance. In this time I also met a girl and entered a relationship. I had some short-term relationships in my teenage years although I couldn't retain my composure. If I was enthusiastic or excited I couldn't hide it, meaning the end. I am also terrible at poker.

Strangely this relationship seemed to work and for the first time I felt like a normal twenty-something embarking on this new stage of my adult life. I had a degree, a girlfriend, and most importantly my Rover 75. We would go for drives in my car on Sundays and go out to dinner like proper adults. I don't think she was too keen on my car; she encouraged me subtly to change it. I didn't part with it until an engine fire destroyed the fuel system. I took the car to a scrap yard, and watching the giant claw grab my car and put it on the pile made me retch. The iron claw smashing through my car windows caused me immediate pain. I grieved for quite some time afterward; such was my attachment to it.

The months passed and I was settling into my new career with relative ease. I was given an opportunity by my recruitment agency to work closer to home, which I gladly accepted. My girlfriend and family were delighted that I was able to work nearer to home, instead of travelling seventy miles to work every day.

I remember taking the time to reflect at how far I had come in life. I was a difficult child that challenged my parents to their absolute limit, yet I had became someone that they could be proud of. Mixing with other children my age certainly helped and the fact that I didn't lead a sheltered existence certainly helped. Mum and Dad had treated me in the same way they planned to had I not had Asperger's. It certainly would have been an easy option to keep me sheltered but they didn't.

I confided to my girlfriend that I had Asperger's and she immediately understood and accepted me for who I was. In previous relationships I had developed a persona and image that collapsed very quickly as time progressed. My social limitations would start to surface and I couldn't hide them. As soon as girls realized that I wasn't the person they thought I was, they left.

I came home from work one evening and my girlfriend told me that she was quite sick. She appeared pale and sad. I asked her what was wrong and she told me she had eaten something bad the previous day and wasn't feeling well at all. I had developed a caring nature and wanted to nurse my stricken girl back to health. The following morning she informed that she felt the same and was quite sick all day.

My naivety didn't allow me to consider the fact that this could potentially be morning sickness. As the days went by, the symptoms of what we hoped was food poisoning were not easing. The sickness was quite bad and she refused to see a doctor or to go to the emergency department. I'm sure at this stage she suspected the reason for her sickness and didn't want to acknowledge what it could have been.

Eventually I remembered a fact I had learned in my first childcare placement: morning sickness was a typical symptom of early pregnancy. In my not-so-subtle way, I decided we should go immediately and find out if we were pregnant or not. We got into the car and drove to a local twenty-four-hour supermarket. We were so afraid that we barely spoke a single word on the way.

A baby—this wasn't part of the plan I had constructed in my head for the remainder of my twenties. I wanted to save to buy us a house, complete a further degree, and study for a PhD to become a lecturer. In my head, a baby would put a spanner in the works, and I didn't know if I had any weapons in my coping arsenal to manage this.

The drive felt like it lasted an eternity. We went in, bought a home pregnancy test, and then sat in silence on the journey back to the house we were living in at the time. Mum and Dad were in Kenya on holiday and I couldn't turn to them for advice and guidance. I was entirely on my own for this one. We looked at each other and she went to perform the test. The anxiety I felt has not been replicated since, nor could it ever be. My girlfriend emerged from the bathroom in tears.

I wasn't sure what the outcome was at this point: tears of relief or tears of sadness? She showed me the test and told me that we were pregnant. I was completely dumbfounded. I couldn't utter a single word nor give her a hug to reassure her. I was stunned. We sat on our bed in disbelief and stayed up late talking about how much a baby was certainly not part of the plan we had for our lives.

I hadn't received news such as this before. My life was going to change forever. Like every first-time parent, I was overcome with dread and doubt. Given my tendency to overthink, this was increased tenfold. I wanted to know immediately what was going to happen over the course of the pregnancy, and not being able to receive answers immediately caused me to become upset and frustrated. When I didn't receive the answers I wanted, I became silent and distant. I had so much uncertainty in front of me and I couldn't cope with it.

I felt up to that point that I was very capable of dealing with situations, but learning I was going to be a father meant the control I craved and needed was taken from me. I wanted to know exactly how things were going to play out and what would happen. Of course none of the situation we found ourselves in was my girlfriend's fault, but I still misconstrued the unknown for her refusing to answer my questions. I felt that I was being ignored, dismissed, and the poor girl didn't even have the answers I was looking for.

Thinking and planning for fatherhood became toxic. I wanted a day-by-day account of how things were, what I could do, and what would happen when the baby was born. I immediately became obsessed, and trying to meticulously plan drove a wedge between us early on in the pregnancy. I hadn't learned to let go of control, and feared so much that my previous vulnerabilities returned. Instead of giving her the comfort and reassurance that she needed, I only wanted to plan. By this stage, she was less than three months pregnant.

When Mum and Dad returned from Kenya, they had barely placed their suitcases on the floor when I told them my news. The look on their faces was one I simply couldn't interpret. Of course they were shocked, although they comforted me and told me they would support me, just like they had done for my entire life. In hindsight, I probably should have told them the following day to allow them to rest after a long journey home.

I remember being in the car with my girlfriend and asking her question after question since my parents were not available. Eventually she became tired of my constant questioning and planning and she became distant. Surely at this stage she hadn't come to terms with being pregnant once again and was full of mixed emotions at the thought of mothering another baby. Shamefully, I didn't see it this way at the time. Instead, I misconstrued her coming to terms with pregnancy as falling out of love with me. Our relationship wasn't the same as it had been and I thought that she didn't love or want me anymore. I just couldn't interpret her emotions any other way and I decided it was best that we parted ways. I reassured her that I would be there for the baby and would attend all appointments with her. We were only together six months and we didn't really know one another terribly well. We were still in our honeymoon period and when this polarized the situation we found ourselves in, I ran. I simply could not cope.

I went from feeling I had conquered the world to feeling vulnerable again in an instant. I had come so far and climbed many mountains, only to have my coping mechanisms fail me at the notion of uncertainty. I had alienated and pushed away my girlfriend, so the certainty I so desperately sought had brought me only more uncertainty, doubt, and further alienation from the people who cared for me. It was going to be a long six months.

CHAPTER 4

I moved back home with Mum and Dad after I left my girlfriend. I hoped that that being back in familiar surroundings would give me some peace to work through my minefield of thoughts. I spent countless hours alone in my old childhood room. I'd lie atop my small single bed, just staring at the ceiling in thought. I certainly feared the worst, not just for myself but also for my unborn baby. I felt as dazed and confused as I did in my earliest days in school.

In somewhat of a paradox, I wanted to know everything that was happening outside the confines of the four walls of my bedroom, yet I never wanted to leave my haven. That baby-blue bedroom witnessed so much of my childhood and early adulthood, from anticipating Santa's arrival to the arrival of my own child and everything in between. I had convinced myself that I was an unfortunate victim of circumstance, as opposed to the master architect of my own downfall. I was very quick to assign blame to others without taking responsibility for my actions and words.

My pregnant ex-partner spoke to me periodically to reassure me that I would play an equal role in the upbringing of our baby, even if we weren't together. Since I had confided to her about my condition, she knew I was prone to overthinking and worrying, but she still didn't wish to see me in person. I don't blame her at all, nor have I ever. My condition didn't excuse what I had ultimately done.

I realize now that my girlfriend's initial shock and sadness at finding herself pregnant again, at such a young age, deeply affected her. I misconstrued this as resentment aimed toward me. In my earliest school days I learned to distance myself from people that I perceived were being nasty toward me. My own safety was my paramount concern and I stuck to this rigidly without exception. My primary concern in my young age was to react if I felt I was being teased or ridiculed. Over time, I decided to avoid conflict and situations I felt were uncomfortable. To the untrained eye, this would surely be seen as cowardice. To me, it was protecting myself.

Mum was working as a family support worker at that time and I was constantly asking her questions. I would repeat the same questions I had asked only a few weeks earlier, until I finally realized that I was getting the same answer to almost everything: I had to wait until the baby was born. I just couldn't accept this. In my mind the appropriate measures that I had wished for had to be in place prior. I needed to know exactly what days I would see him, for how long, and what would take place on those days. I simply couldn't understand the sensitivities that pregnancy brings, the main thing being unpredictability.

I relentlessly kept asking Mum, Dad, and Emily questions. When my parents told me that I would have to wait, I often became aggressive and tearful. I was impossible to live with. Fearing the unknown completely destroyed the excitement of what would ultimately become the greatest blessing in my life.

I would sit up late at night writing out various scenarios and how I would cope with them, one of them being if it was decided that I could not see my baby. I looked up legislation and what rights I would have should this scenario occur. I have to state categorically that this was never even considered by Ethan's mother, and I was always told that I would be able to participate. Despite being told countless times I'd be an active part of my baby's life, I still agonized over all the other possible negative outcomes, making myself sick with worry

I am an emotional avalanche at the best of times. When I am extremely distressed, I cannot prevent showing it to the world. A common misconception surrounding those who live with Asperger's is the lack of emotion and empathy. In my case, I showed a debilitating amount of emotion at both ends of the spectrum. I can become poisonously enthusiastic or infectiously negative. My work colleagues often asked me how I was and I aired my deepest thoughts to anyone who cared to listen. Alienation from almost everyone in my life was becoming a fast reality. Of course, my work performance suffered as well, since I was not sleeping. I was entirely consumed by my situation, one that was entirely my fault.

The coping strategies I had learned through school were based solely on planning my day and making goals and targets. Not being able to set my own goals and targets had become debilitating. I wasn't sleeping, my mood was low, and I spent so much time obsessing and writing in my notepad. I discussed my situation at an appointment with my doctor and I was prescribed medication for the first time.

I remember sitting in the doctor's room, staring at the prescription, and feeling quite sad. It was the first time I realized that my condition would be with me for my entire life; I would never be free from it. I thought I had overcome Asperger's by the time I left university. To me, having Asperger's was a distant memory of a challenge I had faced—one that I had defeated.

I remember pushing through the double doors of the health center, with the prescription in hand, and walking slowly down the street seeing nobody. It was a clear sunny day, but no cars or people passed me. It was almost as if time, space, society, and the universe had completely stopped and I was entirely alone. I couldn't hear a sound. No birds, people, cars, traffic, or life going by. The only thing I could hear were my footsteps shuffling along the pavement.

When I arrived at the pharmacy I didn't want to hand the prescription to the pharmacist. I felt like I had lost, although I couldn't see any other way to keep my emotions under control. By that time, I was only sleeping a handful of hours each night since sleeping interfered with my contingency planning for when my baby was born. Medicating was the only possible path for me to survive the remaining months of the pregnancy

In the coming weeks the medications helped me settle slightly. I was still insufferable to live with, although I did start sleeping much better at night and performing better at work. My work involves working with the most vulnerable in society. People confide in me with their life-limiting illnesses and limitations in order to get the help they so desperately need. During this period in my life, it was hard to hide that I was emotionally frailer than they were, and putting on a positive act was exhausting. I was about to become a parent and was in the prime of my life, but I still lived every day in complete darkness and didn't allow anyone to show me the light. Anyone attempting to focus me on the positives of my life was immediately dismissed.

I had exhausted my parents, especially Mum. She was caring for my grandmother who'd developed dementia and had recently had a debilitating fall at home. Mum moved into my grandmother's home, to better care for her and gain some well-needed respite from me. I tried to offer support as best I could, although I wasn't well myself.

The first ultrasound scan was in February 2013. I was invited to come along and I was delighted. Despite all I had done up to that point, I had been included in this big moment in the pregnancy. We arrived at the hospital and were taken to a small room with the ultrasound scanner. We were both nervous and we were hoping everything was well with the baby. When we saw the first images of our baby up on the screen, we couldn't distinguish any individual features, although we were told all was well. I don't think I said a word during the scan. It still seemed somewhat abstract to me. I didn't know how to feel or act. Should I hold her hand? Should I cry or smile? I just didn't know. This was a situation I had never been in and I felt more confused than anything.

The reality of fatherhood hit home that day. I was terribly worried about the environment my baby would be growing up in—the world I would be bringing my child into. It only seemed a short time ago that I was unable to speak and mix with other children. I was a loner by choice, but I clearly didn't have that choice anymore, because of the responsibility I would have to my child. The autistic child had become an autistic adult, and would soon become an autistic parent.

I was given a picture of the ultrasound scan and I showed it to my parents. That day was almost like a truce. We were happy and excited for the rest of the journey. We talked about buying baby clothes and names we liked, although the darkness and demons in my head were far from gone. I still felt the need to take control of the situation and to plan and know exactly what was to happen from there on.

By March my grandmother was very ill and receiving palliative care. Understandably we were all devastated; our family matriarch was running out of time. My mum had transferred her mother to a nursing home, as her needs could not be met any longer at home, despite all of our best efforts. During this time, Mum was unavailable to listen to my woes and rightfully so. Mum wanted to spend time with her own rock, who had supported her throughout my own challenging upbringing. We all stayed with my grandmother in the nursing home until she passed away at the beginning of April 2013. I was in such a bad state that I didn't even allow my own mother to grieve the loss of her mother properly. I felt so inadequate not knowing how to comfort her.

I was still relentless in my questioning, and my fear of the unknown was still eroding my soul every day. Mum always did her best to reassure me, and my friends often came by to distract me from my worries by taking me fishing. I felt better talking of course, although I spoke too much, and likely annoyed everybody

I did some research into parenting classes, activities, and support for those in the same position as me. I enjoyed formal group settings and benefitted greatly from them in my teenage years. I first thought that if I could just find a group or support network, I might be able to survive those final twelve weeks until the baby was born, but I couldn't find any. I recognize now that I was very ill mentally and a typical antenatal group may not have worked for me, anyway. As I think back on it now, I most likely would have invaded the entire group with my woes, extinguishing the excitement held by the other parents.

At the end of April I was invited to the second ultrasound scan. It was agreed prior that we would find out the gender of our baby so it would help us in our preparations. I was delighted with this decision as it was one detail that I would know. I have never managed well with surprises and I like to prepare. It is a coping mechanism I have kept close to me.

When we saw our baby on the ultrasound screen, he was much bigger and lifelike. He lay casually with his arms behind his head, allowing us to clearly see what gender he was. The nurse didn't even have to tell us. This made us all laugh and it lifted the large atmospheric cloud that I had brought into the room.

Despite how organized I am, I don't tend to keep a record of how often I laugh or smile. I believe that day was probably the only time I laughed throughout the entire pregnancy. We left the appointment smiling and excited at what was ahead for us. She even told me what to buy in anticipation for the birth, such as a stroller, bottle sterilizer, and changing station. I had spent so much time worrying about what would happen when the baby was born that I didn't even think of what equipment I needed. It was quite an expansive list and I needed to get these things immediately.

I told Mum and Dad that they were going to have a grandson and they were delighted. My own grandmother had been so kind and supportive to us throughout her life, and Mum was keen to follow in her example. Mum took me baby-supply shopping and I felt so prepared. We bought little blue clothes and shoes. His shoes were so tiny compared to my Herculean-sized shoes that balance my giant frame. My family found this quite entertaining. This preparing practically comforted me in that I spent less time writing disaster scenarios in my trusty notepad. None of those notepads exist today; I often destroyed them to keep the inner workings of my electrical mind away from public view.

Actually having a list of the things I needed and going to buy them kept me occupied. I bought everything I needed in a matter of weeks and I received donations from family and friends to help me on my way. I finally had a moment of clarity—preparing for the arrival gave me focus and comfort. I had allowed so much time to be consumed by my mind's negative bias that I lost six months of preparation time.

My best advice for anyone coming into a situation like this would be to focus on all that is positive. Had I positively prepared six months prior, I would have been much easier to live with. All the advice I received from my parents was self-interpreted as having to protect myself at all costs. I don't blame them in any way for this, although it did make me process information and situations much more negatively.

It is hard to let go, to come to terms with the unknown, and trying to plan for every single outcome was exhausting. I didn't realize that there were positive things that I could have taken ownership of, such as getting the necessary baby equipment in place. I never considered the equipment I actually would need when the baby came and where to source it. Should I have the ability to reverse time and place myself back in the situation, I would consider what I needed from a practical perspective instead of challenging myself to decipher the unknown.

My trait of trying to plan for every instance had become toxic. I had given myself an impossible task and became frustrated that I wasn't accomplishing anything. I realized that the cat killed by curiosity had died in vain. After this revelation, my mood and daily routine took a positive turn. I started writing lists of what I needed and scoring them out once I had completed them. Although I was taking medication, my mind was still very active, and this was a healthy approach to my constant list-making. I finally was getting to check items off my lists! Finally some happy control.

By June I felt prepared. I had only weeks to go until I would meet my baby boy and anticipation had started to mount. It was decided that I wouldn't be present at the birth and this devastated me at the time. In hindsight, it was probably the correct decision, as I most likely would have donned a gown and gloves and attempted to deliver the baby myself. I was not in a good place and everyone recognized this. We did however decide our baby's name would be Ethan. We both loved the name and were able to agree on this quite easily.

My parent's home was filled with baby things and the weeks were going by so slowly. I was nervous to see how life would change after he was born, but it wasn't affecting me as much as it did in the first three months. I didn't have a toxic view of it anymore and with encouragement from my parents, I let go of the unknown worries . . . somewhat. My room was filled with boxes of toys and baby clothes, and his basket sat proudly beside my bed. Everything was in place. Of course I needed a lot of help from Mum as I didn't know where to start with using everything I had bought.

Excitement started to build for meeting my son. I would see a lot of encouraging parenting quotes on social media along with idyllic photos of smiling parents and their babies. While these can bring comfort and inspire many first-time parents, my fears started to return. Given my analytic mind, I reflected on the last eight months. I had spent at least 80 percent of the time worrying about the unknown and each individual scenario. Yet, the one thing that didn't cross my mind was the reality that my baby could have Asperger's, the same as me.

I never considered that possibility up until that point, that I could have the same journey as my mum and dad had with me. My son could be sneered at, belittled, and made to feel stupid, just as I was. A whole new set of worries flooded me—he may have the same difficult childhood that I had and I wouldn't have the same mindset as my Mother to guide him through it if this was the case. My own anxiety and vulnerability would prevent me from defending him as valiantly as my parents had defended me. The actual cause of Asperger's is unknown, although I feared he could become a victim of genetics.

I only realize now that as all these thoughts and fears took over my mind, I completely regressed back to when I was a child. I didn't really communicate with anybody who wasn't in my immediate family. The processing of the information of becoming a parent became more of a reality with each passing day. The due date was July 23 and as time edged ever closer, the more I needed Mum and Dad for comfort. As I voiced my concerns to them, I wasn't in the frame of mind or even had the ability to process what was being said to me in return. But they would listen to me, and that was all I needed. I can't keep secrets very well and I couldn't keep my feelings inside. It was obvious that my obsessing was upsetting my parents although at the time I didn't realize this. I couldn't interpret their feelings and I was often frustrated that I wasn't receiving the answers that I wanted.

When I was young and learning how to speak, I used cards with facial expressions to help me define feelings. A smiling face card would be attributed to words like *happy* and *laughter*, and with a sad face I would attribute words like *sad* and *upset*. When discussing how I felt, I'd recall the cards, which would then help me structure my words and help me open up about my feelings.

I always thought of the card with the sad face when discussing my worries about becoming a parent. I just didn't know how to verbalize how I felt! How was I supposed to comfort a child when I couldn't translate thoughts into words for so long, and still struggled?

I imagined a scenario of my son coming home upset and being unable to console him. The thought chilled my blood completely. I feared that in time, he would grow to resent me because I wouldn't be like other dads, and that he would be embarrassed or ashamed of me. In truth, I resented myself. I was an outsider who had clung to the coattails of society and somehow managed to survive, but would I survive parenthood?

I decided to buy some parenting books and try looking at some websites. Many of them had visual aids and pictures that I found hard to interpret. I was looking at pictures of babies and they all looked the same to me. All their faces and postures were identical and the descriptions were quite difficult to construe.

The nearest feeling that I can compare it to is the feeling of helplessness one gets when reading the assembly instructions of a piece of furniture. The only difference being is that if one part of the instructions is neglected, it could have a negative impact upon a small baby. So I was quite frightened to say the least.

I learn, read, and process information differently. In an attempt to learn more, I researched support for autistic adults and found very little. Most of the support I discovered was for the parents of autistic children and no resources of support for autistic adults. I know I had my mum to help me, although I wanted to do this on my own simply to prove that I was capable.

I had refused to attend autism-friendly groups because I couldn't imagine many members of the group being in the same situation as me. I failed to realize that despite my situation, my traits and symptoms would have been similar to those in other situations. My brain had processed that I was the only one suffering with the exacerbation of my Asperger's, I felt so alone and that nobody else was like me. I had difficulty processing my own situation and figured nobody would be able to understand. Looking back, I see I could have gained comfort knowing that I wasn't alone in the world. There was no reason I had to face everything entirely on my own, but my ignorance told me that nobody was capable of understanding what I was going through, so I suffered alone.

The trouble with high-functioning autism is the hyper focus on particular sets of circumstances. By twenty-two, I had qualified as a social worker, accumulated wealth, and integrated with other people. The general societal perception of autism includes a lack of independence, complete lack of social skills, and being completely dependent on others for all aspects of daily living. At face value, those closest to me weren't even aware that I had Asperger's.

Asking for and following advice are the hardest things for me to do. If I didn't receive the advice that I felt was right for me, I would toss it aside. It didn't matter to me that people wanted to help. Learning to confide in and appreciate the views of others were things I simply refused to learn to do. I was so confident in my own ability to overcome anything that I didn't feel the need to seek new perspectives.

As much as I would have benefited from additional support at this time in my life, I lacked the ability to follow guidance and apply it to any given situation. A common scenario at work would have been my supervisor trying to give me constructive feedback. I would have started a discussion by asking my boss how they felt it should have been done, we'd discuss their thoughts on the matter, and after an hour or so, "we'd" decide that I was right on all fronts.

In my early twenties I needed to have complete command of a situation. This made me feel confident that the mask I wore to hide any self-believed inadequacies was firmly in place and in no way slipping and giving me away. This is one of the main reasons why I couldn't adjust to healthy feelings toward the pregnancy. I wasn't even the one who was pregnant, yet I refused to listen to the reassurance given to me by everyone.

With only three weeks to go until the due date, another baby scan was scheduled. I had been born with one kidney due to a hereditary defect on Mum's side of the family and this was being investigated with our baby. All was shown to be well and we were both relieved. As I drove my heavily pregnant passenger home after the ultrasound, she asked me how I was doing with everything. Of course I completely lied and told her how strong and mentally capable I was. I told her I had all my things ready and that I had never been more prepared in my life. I know she saw through my façade.

Around this time I was offered a more stable job and I couldn't wait to start. I had various jobs with recruitment agencies that involved a lot of travelling to and from work. This was a boost of good fortune for me. I thought it was certain to stabilize my fledgling career as a social worker. I was also nearby should any childcare issues arise.

Also, right before the birth, my personal doctor requested to see me again for a review of my medications. He felt I had made progress and my mood was certainly much better, albeit not perfect. I was sleeping well at night and was becoming slightly more pleasant to be in the same room with. The medication had worked. Of that there was no doubt. Given the recent public misconceptions about immunizations and medications exacerbating autistic symptoms, I admit to being afraid of using them in the beginning. But knowing what I know now, I urge everyone to accept the help of medications if they are offered. The choice one has to make is between an attempt to feel better or plunging deeper into despair. I chose the former and I'm so glad that I did.

My doctor had also recommended that I participate in some form of talk therapy—cognitive behavioral therapy (CBT) or psychological therapy. At the time, my understanding of those support therapies was that they were for victims of trauma. I didn't realize that I could easily benefit by simply discussing my psychological symptoms. Of course, not being able to see the full reality of my condition, I point-blank refused and didn't want to be characterized as broken, or in any way needing repair.

Throughout the previous eight months, I had isolated myself and often refused to go anywhere with my closest friends. Anytime I did venture out with friends, I'd often want to go home after only just arriving where we were going. It reminded me of being in primary school and not being able to relate to children my own age. I didn't understand them and they didn't understand me. Not being able to relate to anyone my own age was something I hadn't grown out of. I only took comfort from my parents.

Even though my family was still grieving the loss of my grandmother, I couldn't understand their pain. I couldn't understand why people didn't wish to speak to me, and any advice I was given was often discarded. I didn't behave like this without remorse, I just couldn't control how I felt and processed information. I needed reassurance constantly. I often didn't realize the pressure I was putting on others, or what should have been a happy time for me. I had destroyed my own and everyone else's happiness.

My sister decided to help in her own way. She threw me a surprise baby shower party. She decorated her living room with bunting, balloons, and made me a baby hamper. My new hamper contained essentials such as formula, more baby clothes, wipes, and nappies. She realized that I had missed the vast majority of the pregnancy, even if it was my own fault. Emily wanted to enjoy becoming an aunt, as well as helping me feel valued. I received plenty of well wishes although not many knew about how defeated I felt inside.

I settled into the first few days of my new job knowing that my son could arrive any day. I told my new colleagues of my exciting news although it was heavily edited. I didn't tell them that I had fled the scene, cowered in a corner, and obsessively wrote in my notebook for the vast majority of the pregnancy. Under no circumstances were they to discover my vulnerability. I enjoyed my new work but would come home at night and hide in the room I would eventually share with my baby.

During this time, I spent a lot of hours getting to know my new clients and often made myself scarce in the office. I knew that if I remained in the office for too long I would eventually end up saying too much. I was still suffering from over telling my woes to anyone who'd listen and this placed me in a very vulnerable position.

As the birth approached, I found myself scrolling through the pages of one of my many notepads. I had filled it with ridiculous scenarios and my possible solutions to them. I realized none of it mattered and that there would soon be a little person sleeping peacefully in the basket beside my bed. I had work to do. I looked over all his individual items of clothing and imagined them being worn. All the tiny shoes, vests, and T-shirts were arranged and folded neatly into his drawers. I took his entire pram out of the box and attempted to build it in my room. I had all the pieces laid out on the floor and read the instruction manual. Now, if I encounter any difficulties when assembling furniture or other items, I can quickly become frustrated and quit. I attempted to assemble that pram, but after only five minutes, I gave up in defeat. Lucky for me, my dad came upstairs and helped me assemble it. He told me that I would have to get used to building small items of furniture and not to give up so easily. For me this was much easier said than done.

I watched the pram be expertly built by my dad and felt frustrated that I hadn't managed it myself. I was afraid that if I was left alone with complex assembly instructions too long, they were at high risk of being thrown out my bedroom window. Later, my mum showed me how to operate the baby bottle sterilizer, although she may as well have been showing me the flight controls for the Millennium Falcon. I just couldn't focus entirely on the information being given to me.

I awakened to a text message the following day. It was to inform me that my baby was on his way! His due date was July 23, 2013, and I received a message at 7 AM that morning. My son's arrival on his due date confirmed to me that he was indeed his father's son.

CHAPTER 5

The due date was finally upon us and emotions were mixed as Mum, Dad, and I sat in the living room of our house. We knew the baby was coming and we sat in solemn silence for the vast majority of the day. Mum and Dad were most likely terrified of what was ahead for all of us in the coming days.

While I had shown signs of improvement, changes of circumstances always yielded negative consequences for everyone. They were likely preparing for the daunting task of helping me come to terms with being a parent and all the responsibility that comes with it.

In their eyes I had just learned how to speak and navigate the world semi-independently. I still needed support from them, and I always will, but this was a change for them too. They were becoming grandparents for the first time. It crossed my mind that they had helped me through so many battles and this was just the next one. They had prevented me from going to a school that I didn't need to go to, had taught me how to speak, and now they had the unenviable battle of teaching me how to parent.

Looking back, those past nine months seemed to go by so quickly. All my planning and note writing consumed all of my time. But for Mum and Dad, time likely stood agonizingly still.

While sitting in my parent's living room, waiting for word from the hospital, the world stood still again. I couldn't hear the TV, couldn't hear my parents talking, nothing passed by the window, and all I could feel were my lungs inflating and deflating. In the brief moments when the world did come back to me, I would check my phone to see if there were any updates. Time moved agonizingly slow that day.

To pass the time, I ended up calling my sister to tell her we were all at home waiting for the baby to arrive, and that all was well. It had been several hours since I received the text telling me that the baby was on the way and I started to feel excited. That day wasn't governed by fear and planning. All I wanted to know was that the delivery was a success. Whether I had accomplished the impossible task of planning for all the unknown in the months prior no longer mattered. I just wanted the baby to be well and greeted with happiness from all of us.

I even rehearsed holding him for the first time in my room. I treated meeting my baby for the first time like an interview. Like all social interactions, I found this one challenging. What were the first words I would speak to my baby? How would I hold him? What do I say to everyone? In most scenarios I like to visualize an event. I visualize my entrance, opening lines, and how I'll steer the conversation in my favor to integrate smoothly. This is how I have always coped as an adult.

I tried to visualize what was going on in the hospital. I actually didn't have a proper account of that day's events until recently and I was quite shocked to hear how it went. Ethan's mum told me how the day unfolded in the knowledge that I was writing this book.

She was at home with her parents when her body told her that the baby was coming. She went immediately to the hospital, accompanied by her mother. It was very early in the morning with a bright blue sky, a rare occurrence in Ireland. The day was very cold, I remembered that much.

When Ethan's mum arrived at the hospital, the medical team discovered that Ethan was in a complicated position in the womb and that delivery would not be easy. Labor was very slow and not much happened over the course of the day, while I sat at home staring at my shoes in anticipation. It wasn't until 4 PM that things really started moving along. Contractions were getting more frequent and pain was increasing. When looking at Ethan on the ultrasound monitor, the obstetrician and the midwives were quite concerned. He wasn't in a natural position and they didn't know the best way to proceed. If I had been present, I would have had a meltdown. I wouldn't have been able to process this and would have demanded an answer to this complex medical dilemma on the spot. I wouldn't have helped matters in the slightest nor would I have been able to handle this emotional situation.

Ethan's life was very much in danger and the risk of complication was increasing as the minutes ticked by. A decision had to be made to deliver naturally or perform an emergency caesarean section. Natural birth would place him at risk for asphyxiation due to his head being placed higher in the womb and the umbilical cord close to his neck. And a caesarean section incision would have been too close to his head.

An impossible decision was being discussed by the medical team and all Ethan's mum could do was wait in despair. She told me her mum kept her composure and was able to comfort her and help prevent any unnecessary stress. Labor wasn't moving forward any more quickly and a decision needed to be made sooner rather than later. Inducing the later stages of labor also increased the risk of fetal asphyxiation given Ethan's position.

All while this was occurring, time was moving slowly for me from the comfort of my living room. I can't imagine how slowly it was moving inside that hospital room that day.

From my parents' home, I could actually see the hospital. We only lived about mile away and it was visible through the cherry blossom tree in our back garden. From time to time I would look in that direction and wonder what was going on. But I had no idea at the time how critical things were.

It came to 4:30 PM and I hadn't heard anything. I started to fear that the baby had been born and I hadn't been informed yet. I think Mum and Dad had started to become nervous too.

At 5 PM the medical team arrived at the decision to proceed with a natural birth and that a Caesarean wasn't the safest option given the circumstances. Ethan would need to come in to the world quickly if he were to have a fighting chance. Preparations for surgery would have cost vital minutes that neither Ethan nor his mum had.

I was at home staring at my phone from 5 PM onward. Every time my phone rumbled in my pocket I immediately leapt to my feet to see if it was a progress update from the hospital. I remember a friend texting me to wish me well and muttering to my parents that it was only a well-wisher and no further news.

As the birth progressed complications became apparent very quickly. His position was not changing and his heart rate began to fall dramatically. Ethan's grandmother had a nursing background and was able to assist practically during the birth. A crisis situation developed and Ethan's chances of surviving the birth were getting lower. The situation they faced was becoming dire and his umbilical cord was beginning to wrap around his body.

The midwives and obstetrician had to act quickly to change his position in order to give him his best chance of survival. Attempting to manipulate his position in the womb in active labor caused considerable pain and I can't even attempt to comprehend what this was like.

By 5:30 we were all concerned. My mum and dad are usually the epitome of calm and tranquility. I would like to compare their strength to diamonds, although diamonds are weak and brittle compared to them. Mum and Dad wore what I perceived to be quite worried faces. When reading facial expressions I always revert back to the face cards from my earliest education. Both of their faces matched the card with the worried expression.

Like dominoes, when they worried, the operation collapsed entirely. I became distressed and my parents had to prevent me from busting through the front door and running the short mile over to the hospital. They urged me to calm and I must state categorically that no one in the history of being told to calm down has calmed down.

Meanwhile back at the hospital, the medical team struggled to make any significant progress and Ethan's heart rate was struggling to increase from thirty-five beats per minute. I was told that an entire medical team was present, as well as several midwives and a surgical team. The room was extremely crowded and frantic. I can't imagine being there to see it. Even now writing this, I am unsure as to how I would have attempted to make sense of the situation.

Every time my phone made a noise, my heart would skip several beats. At 6:10 PM my phone rang and this time it wasn't a false alarm. The name on the screen was Ethan's mum's brother. I nervously answered the phone and he told me that Ethan had been born at 6:01 PM and that all was well. My immediate reaction was complete shock. Not only had the day come, but the moment had come with it.

Mum drove me over to the hospital and left me at the entrance in order to find a parking space. I barely knew where to go and I had to nervously request directions to the labor ward from reception. When holding my hand outward to press the lift button, I felt my hands contract. In times of extreme nervousness, my whole body becomes rigid and I hold a fixed and sad stare.

The lift took approximately three years to come to the ground floor and I couldn't get any sense of composure whatsoever as I waited.

I stepped inside and embarked on another three-year journey to my destination. I remember taking steps forward toward the entrance to the labor ward, yet the more steps I took, the farther away the door seemed to become.

I approached one of the midwives and informed them that my baby had just been born. She told me that mother and baby were receiving aftercare, postnatal checks, and that I would have to wait until this was finished. I sat in a hard wooden chair beside the nurse's station and I tried to absorb my surroundings. The noise of crying babies and the beeping of medical equipment made me feel very uneasy. When I go to the hospital now to visit a client, I get the same nervous feeling when I hear beeping machines.

In childhood when noises were too loud I covered my ears. I would feel my hands rise up as if I had no control over them and would place my palms as hard as I could against my ears. As I waited in that lobby, my hands began to involuntarily lift toward my ears. It was unsettling to me and added on top of the nerves I was already experiencing in prospect of meeting my baby for the first time.

But before my hands reached my ears a nurse called out my name. Immediately the noise of the ward disappeared and I stared at the nurse with vulnerable anticipation. My mum hadn't arrived yet and I wanted her to be with me when I met Ethan for the first time. My logic at the time was for her to keep a watchful eye over me so that I could take comfort from her. I could barely stand up as my body had contracted more when sitting down. I fought the urge to vomit and proceeded down the corridor to the room Ethan had been born in.

I walked through the door and saw my little boy all wrapped up and cozy in his mother's arms. His eyes were closed and he was asleep given the tough day he'd had. He looked so small and peaceful. I fell in love immediately and couldn't stop looking at him. I sat in the chair beside the bed and stared with wonder. I didn't say a word when I entered the room and I remember his mum asking me if I wanted to hold him. She placed him on my lap and showed me how to hold him properly, supporting his tiny head since he couldn't hold it up himself. I had rehearsed my opening speech to my son but I didn't have a breath to say any words.

He lay in my arms completely content. For the next few minutes all the worries and anguish of the preceding months vanished. It was the first time in my life I had felt completely at peace and didn't feel the pressure of how others viewed me in that particular moment. Simple emotions are quite tough for me at the best of times, but love was a completely different story. I wish I could describe that feeling I had when I was holding him for the first time, but I just can't.

While I was holding him, he stared to wake. His mum and I shared a look of awe as his eyes opened. I took him over to the window. The room he was born in had a scenic view that stretched for miles in the distance. We immediately bonded over my love of staring out of windows and I immediately couldn't imagine what my life was like without him. I felt the man holding the baby was not the man who'd entered the room.

When Ethan started to squint because of the bright light, I moved back to the chair. I held out my finger and Ethan clasped on to it. This moment was captured on his mum's phone and I have since had it printed on canvas. It is not currently on display in my house as Ethan feels embarrassed by it and demanded I take it down. He dislikes photographs of himself as a baby, another personality trait that proves he is his father's son. He continued to hold on to my finger for some time, his little brain making sense of the chaotic world around him after having spent nine months in peace and tranquility. We deeply connected at the confusion of the world around us.

While I held Ethan I felt my phone rumble in my pocket—it was Mum. She was so excited and she wanted to come up to the room and meet her grandson. Mum and Emily arrived and the atmosphere in the room was so positive. Mum and Emily took turns holding our new bundle of joy and he kept his eyes open to greet them, too. Both sides of the family had come together to welcome Ethan into the world. I was always worried that I would have been admonished by everyone involved for what I had done in the months leading up to the birth. When we all finally met Ethan, none of that mattered. Ethan drifted in and out of slumber throughout the short time we were there. Given the traumatic birth for Ethan and his mum, the obstetrician and the midwives wanted to carry out further tests and examinations. It was time to go. I didn't want to leave Ethan and go back home. My mum reminded me that the day had been quite difficult for them and that it was best to allow them time to rest and process what had happened throughout the day. At the time I didn't know what had taken place and I felt annoyed that I was asked to leave so soon. I gave Ethan a final embrace before handing him back to his mum. We were so excited and my mum shed a tear in the car on our way home. Seeing people crying can confuse me greatly. I didn't know if they were tears of joy or tears of sorrow for what she knew was ahead.

I returned to the haven of my room to try to make sense of the events that had taken place over the course of that day. I was now a father! That was the most difficult thing to process. I was now responsible for another human life, but also needed so much support for myself. I was satisfied that Ethan was well, but I had a feeling of dread for what the following weeks and months held in store.

At 11 PM I received a text with a picture of Ethan sleeping in an incubator. It's strange how seeing that photo of Ethan ended up being the antidote to my fears. He had allowed me to hold him without tears. During that short time together, we had bonded silently in the chaotic world we would have to navigate together. He was a stranger to the world and so was I, after all, we were embarking on a great unknown journey.

I looked around my bedroom, which, over the weeks, had been completely transformed into a nursery for Ethan. I couldn't wait to have bonding time with him in this room that I'd made for him. I had always been very cautious about my own personal space in the past and seldom allowed anyone to share it with me. This had doomed friendships, work relationships, and even romantic relationships. When Ethan was born, I couldn't wait to bring him into my world and show him everything I had. I didn't even allow my parents to rummage through my things (I could be very protective of my living and working spaces.) As I sat in my room that night, I didn't have any foreboding fear that Ethan would soon be sharing my space.

I slept soundly that night and received a call from the hospital in the morning. Ethan and his mum were to be discharged that afternoon. It was agreed that they would stay with Ethan's maternal grandmother for the first few weeks in order to aid recovery and rest. So Ethan, along with his mum and grandmother, left the hospital at 10 AM on the 24th of July. I was invited to go and visit later that evening.

I couldn't wait to see Ethan again although I hadn't planned for the postnatal circumstances we found ourselves in. I hadn't imagined having to visit him where he was and I didn't feel prepared. It wasn't a scenario I'd worked through and was nervous and obviously excited— I couldn't wait to leap into my car and drive right over.

When I walked through their front door, the sounds of crying greeted me and lead me to Ethan. He had prepared a welcoming gift for my arrival—a very pungent gift indeed! As this would be my first time changing a nappy, Ethan's mum was incredibly gracious and allowed me to change him. My negative bias throughout the pregnancy had led me to plan for ridiculous scenarios, but not for something so practical as the task of changing my son's dirty nappy.

Here I stood having researched every article and book on the subject of parental rights to the point where I could recite them. I even could have presented wonderfully in the European Court of Human Rights, yet, I hadn't researched how to change a baby after the "business" was done!

My senses are heightened at the best of times and my wonderfully different brain had not prepared for the olfactory overload that befell me. As I unraveled Ethan's tiny paper underwear, I received my official welcome to the parenting party. Despite my protests and threats of vomit, Ethan's mum refused to allow me to give up. Ethan's blood-curdling screams did not help matters. I couldn't place my hands over my ears while changing him. Or hold my nose! I have always had sensory issues and I didn't consider the struggles I would face once he was born. Between his loud cries and soiled nappies, I didn't know if I would manage.

Even now, if a pub is too loud, I often end up standing outside to have breaks from the noise and allow my mind to clear. I realized in that moment that with a baby, I couldn't do that. I had to face this challenge for Ethan.

The following day, Ethan's mum was exhausted, so she called to request that I take him for a few hours so she could have a rest and I could spend quality time with him. I was delighted to be able to show him our home and all the things that I had prepared for him. I couldn't operate a car seat when I arrived, so his mum showed me how to tuck him into the car seat. As I pulled out of the driveway, I refused to leave second gear. I didn't want to disturb his slumber and I drove very slowly for the five-mile journey to my house.

When we got home Mum was ready with her camera. She took so many photographs and I enjoy looking back on that day often. My parents adore him and held him for the majority of the time. I took him to our room and showed him all of our things. I explained the order of the room to his sleeping face and requested that he not disturb it too much as everything was orderly!

My mum stood over me to ensure I operated Ethan's bottle sterilizer and changed his clothes properly. With practice and guidance I felt competent. After such a successful first visit, Ethan's mum agreed I could continue to care for him for several hours each day. And only after several weeks, I was allowed to finally keep him overnight. I was delighted to have a sleepover with him so we could bond. I laid him into his basket that night and he fell asleep like an angel. I hadn't been told that Ethan had developed colic, though, and slept very little that night. While I was sleeping the baby bomb exploded. Ethan wailed and cried through the night and I was stunned! While Ethan was crying I didn't know what to do. I held him and wanted to do everything I could to soothe him back to sleep. I decided that he didn't like me and I took his crying personally. Despite being fed, changed, and winded, he continued to be upset. Mum shuffled into our room and offered to help me. I was quite agitated by this point and wanted to be able to soothe him to sleep myself, but I couldn't, so Mum told me to go back to bed as I had work in the morning and that she was happy to help.

I couldn't sleep. I lay staring at my ceiling, doubting myself. I couldn't even soothe my own child back to sleep. I thought I wasn't good enough and feared Ethan could sense that I was different. Could a baby several weeks old realize something about Daddy wasn't right?

By the time Ethan was born I was fully aware of the battles Mum and Dad faced with me as a child. When a health visitor came to visit Ethan and I, she inquired if autism or developmental delay ran on either side of the family. I quickly said no! I had decided that I was somehow capable of accelerating Ethan's developmental milestones and attempted to teach him how to speak. I sat him on my lap facing me and spoke to him. Most of my speaking lessons resulted in Ethan giggling, crying incessantly, or falling asleep.

I constantly sat him on my knee and spoke to him. I feared he wouldn't be able to speak or verbalize to me. I believed that Ethan needed to learn to speak early since facial expressions were still a weakness for me. I pointed to pictures in bright books and explained everything to him. He stared at me blankly and didn't verbally respond. He was preoccupied with the bright colors and the pop-up pictures. I believe I may be the only person in history to read Hamlet to a four-month-old baby.

As a gift, Mum arranged for professional photographs to be taken when Ethan was six months old. By this point, I kept him overnight frequently and his colic had eased considerably (that is until his teeth started to appear). I was changing Ethan's clothes for the photographer in our living room when he said his first word, *Dada*! I ran upstairs with my partially clothed baby to tell my sleeping parents my news. They were delighted and the professional photographs from that day are a reminder of when Ethan said his first word. This was a glimmer of hope for me that Ethan didn't have Asperger's, too. I had been so worried about Ethan having the same condition as me, along with all the difficulties I faced. I felt deep down I wouldn't be able to fight for him in the same way that my parents did for me.

By Ethan's first birthday, he was making progress on being able to walk and I was able to converse with him freely. His vocabulary was exceptional for his age and this was a huge relief for me. In fact, his vocal range was much better than mine and he was meeting his developmental milestones with ease. In comparison, I had been nowhere near walking or speaking when I was a year old. His first birthday party came and I wondered where the year had gone. Ethan and I had a very solid routine down and he slept and ate at the same times throughout the day. He was sleeping much better at night and I knew what to expect on a daily basis, which suited me greatly given my love of the known.

My senses had adapted to Ethan, becoming much more tolerant. I was able to soothe him if he was upset and I even tolerated changing his nappies. He called me Daddy and I loved hearing it. It was surreal and hard to process for a long time, that I was someone's father. Ethan had fitted seamlessly into my life. I was also enjoying my work every day and loved showing my colleagues pictures of him. Mum and Dad were proud of how I had coped during that first year of Ethan's life. I had a sense of order that made me feel at peace.

Around this time, I received a call from my doctor asking to see me. He wanted to review my medication and compliance. I told the doctor I was taking my medications every morning, although I was in such a good place that I felt they were no longer needed. He explained to me that the medication can take twelve to fifteen months to have a full effect and I should remain on the medication to keep my mind and thoughts stable. I agreed to maintain my medications, but soon afterward I made a mistake. I decided that my doctor was wrong and that I didn't need to remain medicated for my condition.

I was on top of the world. My son was happy, I was happy, and my parents were happy. I didn't plan and overthink as much as I used to. For once I felt somewhat normal and I had never felt normal before. My relationship with Ethan was strong and I was able to take Ethan for walks in the park without feeling like I stood out from the crowd. I had spent my entire life attempting to become part of the crowd and now felt as if I was like any other person. Of course, I devised the trips to the park and the daily routine that we lived by, but lucky for me, Ethan fitted seamlessly into this life I had constructed. At just one year old, he'd learned my way of working and what to expect.

I was able to plan our days together and I had comfort from knowing what to expect from each passing day. By October, Ethan was happy to explore the world on his own two feet and he was able to recognize animals he saw. My sister also learned that she was expecting a baby around this time and Ethan loved to rub her baby bump. Ethan had boundless energy that I was able to keep up with. He also loves swimming and I began taking him to the swimming pool when he was only a few months old. When we go on holiday now, he remains in the pool for the entire time.

When Christmastime came along, Ethan and I decided to go to town to buy gifts and visit Santa. He had no idea who Santa was and I was keen to tell him all about Santa on the way there. But, when he saw Santa he became terrified and wanted to leave, so we went shopping. We were standing in a line waiting to pay for our items when a larger lady came up and stood in the line behind us. She smiled and gave a friendly wave to Ethan. I didn't know who this person was and she was only politely greeting my ray of sunshine, but Ethan responded by pointing to her midsection and uttering, "Baby?" Horrified, I immediately grabbed Ethan and reprimanded him. Luckily the lady took no insult and found this extremely amusing, even laughing loudly. She asked if someone close to us was expecting and I nodded in agreement before dragging Ethan out of the shop. That wasn't part of the very planned script I ran our lives by and I didn't know how to manage the situation. Instead, I fled the shop with Ethan as if I had robbed it and went home empty-handed. (I decided to go another time without Ethan present.) Of course this instance was taken in good humor, although I wasn't able to deal with the situation. While it is a witty anecdote now, it was deeply embarrassing for me at the time.

Whenever we ventured out in public together, I'd find it difficult to talk to people spontaneously. When on an outing, I knew from the moment we set off in the car what our plan of attack would be. We would arrive at our destination, do what we needed to do, and go home. That was my predetermined sequence and any changes to that unsettled me greatly, especially when we ran into people I knew.

Christmas passed and my parents convened a meeting with me in their living room. They were so pleased at how Ethan was progressing and how I was adapting to being a parent. They knew I had savings and offered to assist me in buying my own home. I was delighted at this offer and couldn't wait to go house hunting. Ethan and I would have our own place to call home and create new memories in—both good and bad.

CHAPTER 6

The time had come for Ethan and me to find a home of our own. Ethan had lived between his mum's house and our family home for his first eighteen months. I had only lived alone once, during my time at university, but I had struggled and eventually moved back home after only six months. Before my first attempt at living on my own, I was used to following an already-established routine, the one Mum had in place for the house. I wasn't confident enough to establish a routine of my own during my university years but that had now changed.

While living at home with my parents, I'd become familiar with Ethan's routine. He awakened every morning around 7 AM and had breakfast. Mum would then come downstairs and entertain him when I left for work at 8:30. He had an early lunch followed by a nap at midday that often lasted until 2 PM. He then went on adventures with Mum or Dad until I returned from work for dinner at 5:30 PM. After dinner he got changed into his pajamas, had a bedtime story, and was asleep by 7 PM. His routine was the same when he was with his mum. On the weekends I took him on adventures and he often went back to his mum on a Saturday evening or Sunday evening on alternate weeks.

Ethan, like all children nowadays, was mesmerized by our mobile phones and tablets. I often sat with him and looked at houses that I could afford. My budget wasn't very big although I could tell Ethan had expensive taste. He would often ask if we could have a house with a swimming pool. Any houses I saw within my budget were modest and in need of repair. When I showed them to Ethan he often said he didn't like them. This was the start of my struggles with parenthood. I took everything he said literally and personally. I felt like a failure because I couldn't buy an outrageous home complete with a swimming pool.

After weeks of searching for a house I eventually found one that I liked. It was situated in a quiet street adjacent to the river. It was placed comfortably in the middle of a row of terraced houses that were built in the 1890s and was painted a bright shade of magnolia. The house had a large living room that led into the kitchen, and the bathroom located just off the kitchen through a small door. This house had history— many feet had tread upon those old wooden floorboards before Ethan and I made it our home. The carpet on the narrow curved staircase was tired and worn. Upstairs had two large bedrooms, one overlooking the river and the other facing the rear alley behind the house.

It was small, located near the city center, and I loved the view from what would be my bedroom window. I imagined myself staring out my bedroom window at the river and the hills beyond the city. I brought Ethan to view the house with me and he loved the huge living room—he even told me where he'd store all his toys. I conferred with him about purchasing the property and he emphatically insisted we buy the house immediately. He carefully navigated the steep staircase to the two bedrooms. He also loved the view from river-facing bedroom window and he attempted to hoist his flag in my room. I had decided that the view was too pretty for an eighteen-month-old to appreciate and I relegated him to the rear bedroom.

We were both excited and decided to purchase the house. Our estate agent was very accommodating and agreed to help us move in as quickly as possible. I knew exactly how I wanted the house to be set up and had already designed the layout of things while touring it. I knew the house needed repairs and I was keen to begin as soon as I moved in.

We moved into our new home in March 2015. Mum and Dad were delighted that I was moving out because it demonstrated that I was quite independent. I was able to cook, operate a washing machine, and iron clothes. Mum could very easily have completed everything for me to the point where dependence was established, but instead she exposed me to the real world in small, manageable doses. I enjoyed learning how to be my own man. I was excited about taking control of my life and I felt ready to take on the world with Ethan by my side.

I was on such a tight budget that I often opted for secondhand furniture or donations from family and friends. My house was a collage of mismatching patterns and designs. It was perfect. I struggle with patterns and color schemes, so my chosen décor was based on what made me feel comfortable at the expense of being aesthetically pleasing. We ate our meals at a wobbly glass table, sat in worn furniture, and wore extra layers to compensate for the archaic heating system. We were in our element!

I often felt lonely when Ethan went back to his mum's house, and I would organize his toys and the rest of the house to keep myself occupied. I'd put his crayons back in the boxes and make up his bed for his eventual return. I came home one evening and started to arrange my cutlery drawer in my kitchen. I had returned home at 5 PM and after spending what seemed only a few minutes organizing my knives, forks, and teaspoons, it was suddenly 11:40 PM. I found this very bizarre and I felt very perplexed. I wouldn't describe this as a blackout—I was aware of what I was doing. As the weeks went by I had more incidents of obsessing without realizing so much time had passed. I spent hours folding towels, arranging my food cupboards, and planning my week ahead. I thought my obsessive planning trait had left me!

In work, I started to do the same. I took a file from my filing cabinet to file a report that had been posted to my office. After what seemed to be just a few minutes, a colleague asked to speak to me in private and asked if I was well. I confirmed that I was and he looked puzzled. Little did I know that I had spent five hours organizing one client file and had missed my lunch break. When I realized the time, I lied and said the file was a mess. I spent so much time obsessing that time was racing ahead without me. My colleagues believed I was a confident force of nature that took everything in stride and they were right. So what was the difference? I had stopped taking my medication eight weeks prior. My colleagues started to suspect something was seriously wrong with me. They apparently had thought so for months.

In keeping with time disappearing from me, it was Ethan's second birthday. Ethan's mum and I decided to have the birthday party at my house, and he was showered with gifts. As it was his second birthday, I was frequently told about the dreaded "terrible twos," when behavioral issues would become apparent. Little did I know that my own behavioral issues and traits were beginning to return ever so slowly with each passing day, too. After the birthday party, we took Ethan and all his party guests to a local indoor play area. I had been there with him many times before but this visit would be entirely different. When I led Ethan by the hand through the door I was caught completely by surprise. The lights of the arcade games started to sting my sensitive eyes, the din of children playing caused me to squirm, and the smell of different foods colliding nauseated me. I started to feel nervous and I wanted to hide in my car.

When all the children gathered at the soft play area, I excused myself from my guests and went to the bathroom. I closed the stall door behind me and stood quietly. I was sweating profusely, and without warning, my hands left my sides and started creeping upward toward my ears. This hadn't happened to me for two years. I closed my eyes, but I could still see the dancing colors of the arcade machines. Being away from the lights, noise, and smells brought little relief and I realized that I was in the middle of a meltdown. I knew if I was gone too long, the party guests would suspect something was wrong. After channeling all of my mental strength, I forced my hands from my ears and opened the stall door.

I returned to the play area and looked at my mum. She had a very concerned look and asked me how I was. I told her I had eaten something that didn't agree with me. She didn't question this and I couldn't interpret from her face if she believed me or not. The party ended after what seemed an eternity and I was finally able to drive home. I arrived around 6 PM and went straight to bed. I slept until my alarm the following morning.

I acknowledged that these can happen from time to time, but I also couldn't remember the last sensory meltdown I'd had. I hadn't thought I needed medication anymore. My rationale being that those with epilepsy can still suffer from seizures despite medication compliance. I had progressed so well and decided to view this as a minor setback. I will always remember the feeling of confusion on my school playground all those years ago. That day I felt exactly the same. I was an adult hosting my child's birthday party—I couldn't disengage from the situation and stand with someone who gave me comfort.

Ethan came and went between his two homes, but he had recently started spending every weekend with me. He arrived home with me one particular weekend and all was well on Friday evening. He went to bed with little issue and enjoyed his bedtime story before fading off to sleep. The clockwork routine was still in place and I went downstairs to watch TV or read. After some time I noticed a figure out of the corner of my eye. I turned to see Ethan standing in the living room, having not heard him come down the stairs. My perception was that he was supposed to sleep the entire night. This wasn't part of the script for the evening. He was holding his bear and staring at me blankly. I had no idea how to react. This was a change in his routine and I asked him what was wrong. He didn't answer. I carried him back upstairs to his room, but he refused to get back into bed. I couldn't understand what was happening. We ended up venturing back downstairs and he sat beside me on the sofa with his bear. I felt so confused since his routine was set, but now he had changed it. He eventually did go back to bed after about an hour, but this change haunted me for the rest of the night.

Occasionally, Ethan would rise early in the morning, but now he was starting to rise between 5:30 and 6 AM. I was so used to hearing him call my name at 7 AM and once again, he was altering the order of our day. If I was waking for work earlier than my pre-programmed 7 AM start, I couldn't adjust for the remainder of the day. When I arrived at my office I felt like a child that had dropped an ice cream or lost a balloon. I couldn't recover emotionally from the slightest of cracks in routine. Between losing time obsessing over client files and not recovering from my fluctuating waking times, my colleagues started asking questions. I told them I was up all night or that I wasn't well. I never told the truth. I misconstrued their genuine concern for suspicion and feared my cover was blown. I started to look for other jobs.

Ethan's sleeping pattern showed no signs of stabilizing and my days were often different and not following my carefully planned routine. This didn't suit me at all. I phoned my mum and asked her why Ethan was deciding to wake up at different times. I couldn't understand why he slept soundly in the past but decided to change now. Mum told me that this was a perfectly natural behavior and it was of no concern whatsoever. This was no consolation to me since I couldn't handle changes in routine back then. I started to feel as if Ethan's waking habits were my fault and decided to discover why this was happening. I spent many hours on my phone trying to obtain a suitable answer. Now I know that my processing skills had deteriorated without me realizing and the issue wasn't Ethan's sleeping pattern, it was my ability to cope with changes in the routine.

I eventually adapted somewhat and came to "forgive" Ethan for waking at different times over the course of several months. He was verbalizing well and he was a happy and excited two-and-a-half-year-old. He loved playing games and drawing pictures for me. He learned to use the toilet with relative ease with his mum's help, and he was so proud of himself (and so was I). He was growing up so quickly while I, on the other hand, was regressing back to the traits I thought I'd left behind. Even during his toilet training, I couldn't receive advice nor could I process information provided to me. If I encountered a challenge I felt defeated if I didn't find it easy.

As time went by, Ethan started to refuse some of his favorite foods. This was another change for me that I couldn't understand. I made him the same meal repeatedly hoping that I had made it wrong and that he would eat it. He still refused. I called Mum to share my new dilemma. I told her that Ethan wasn't eating what he usually enjoyed and that there must be some reasoning behind it. Again Mum explained that as children develop, their appetites often vary. She told me that I survived eating plain biscuits with glasses of milk for four years. She reminded me that as I grew up, my diet started to vary again, and the same would most likely happen with Ethan. Of course, this was no consolation and I insisted his mum and I consult a doctor. We were told that most children have a reduced appetite in their second year as the taste buds and swallow reflex develop. In my view, this had to be wrong. I thought he wasn't eating because he didn't want to accept what I was serving him and that I was a failure as a father. I was once again reverting back to taking everything personally and couldn't see the situation for what it really was, nor did I want to.

One day, Ethan's mum called and asked if I was well. I told her that I was concerned about Ethan and that he wasn't having a regular sleep pattern or eating like he used to. She reassured me that she had seen these behavioral changes before with her daughter, and he would mature beyond them. I didn't admit to her that I felt it was my fault. I couldn't get my brain to think any other way.

In addition to the changes at home to my carefully cultivated routine, there were operational changes at work and I struggled with these. Changes to paperwork, visiting schedules, or ways of working can greatly trouble me. I was still able to carry out my duties albeit with a dark cloud hovering over my head. I was able to visit people with my pre-planned friendly demeanor and portray that all was well with the world. I had to act fine to avoid suspicion. I still don't know to this day if I succeeded. I continued to keep my focus at work although I wanted to pursue another job elsewhere. I know it's strange that while change frightened me so much, during this time I wished to run and seek another change. It's an autistic paradox that I hope some readers will understand.

The time had come to move to another job. I had accepted a position thirty miles from home since it came with a permanent contract. In my first three years as a social worker I had gone from place to place while on temporary contracts. This was my first permanent contract. I gladly accepted as I felt the permanent contract would bring the stability I so desperately needed.

At no stage during all these changes in my life did I consider visiting a doctor. I didn't believe a doctor could magically make me a better parent and that having Asperger's had nothing to do with the challenges

I was suddenly facing again. Many of my teenage and adult struggles were my own making and so I had mistaken the natural development of my child to be my fault. I knew my mood had become poor, but I didn't want to admit defeat and ask for help. I wanted to attempt to overcome my parenting struggle on my own. I was calling Mum incessantly to ask her why Ethan wasn't eating, sleeping, or following routine like he used to. Mum and Dad often refused to retell advice they had already given me and confronted me often. I of course didn't listen to them. They tried to help me and I wouldn't take any of the advice they gave me. I didn't want to feel helpless and I wanted to stand on my own two feet.

It was October 2015 and I was leaving to start my new job. My work colleagues bought me a gift and took me out for lunch on my last day. I suspect they knew there was plenty going on inside my head and out-side of work that they were not aware of. I couldn't risk anyone finding out how my life really was. Given my professional position, I didn't know how people would react if they knew I was on the autistic spectrum. I believed that it might compromise my job prospects and career oppor-tunities. Despite my many woes, I enjoy my work and enjoy helping others. It's even a little funny how I was able to give sound advice without being able to take any advice myself.

Taking a new job in another town was a fresh start for me, although hopelessly impractical. If I was ever asked to take care of Ethan at the spur of the moment, I couldn't. I was thirty miles away working in a busy team specializing in dementia care. My new colleagues were very welcoming as were the managers. I seemed to fit in quite well and enjoyed going there. The team included both social workers and psychiatric nurses. I wasn't fully aware of this before I accepted the position and despite their friendliness, I felt worried. Could they see through my carefully sculpted mask and persona? My guess, given their bundles of knowledge and professionalism, is that they did.

I was working so far away that my parents had to care for Ethan on the days he was supposed to be with me. I often left for work at 7:45 AM and Ethan stayed with them until I returned home, often after 6 PM. I spent the weekend days with him, although some weeks he was seeing very little of me. In some ways, I came to terms with this because I was sensing Ethan was starting to become aware that I was different. I thought he was better off spending time with the stable people in his life. Mum and Dad were starting to notice that I was reverting back to my old ways but couldn't speak to me about it because I was so unreasonable. It didn't matter what they said; I was mistaking constructive criticism for judgment and would became upset. I couldn't see any way for the vicious cycle to end.

I would always become nervous when returning home at night. I was afraid that Ethan wouldn't want to come with me. Often when I collected him from my mum and dad, he didn't want to leave them. I know now that his days with Mum and Dad included an extra biscuit or an extra ten minutes watching TV. They spoiled him and rightfully so. They informed me that it was their role as grandparents, but I felt Ethan didn't like our house anymore or any of our things.

Ethan spent the majority of our time together wishing to return to his mum or back to my parents. I often gave in to his demands or I'd purchase his friendship through ice cream or toys. The persona I had developed throughout my life caused distances between me and those I care about. I was used to this and accepted it. With Ethan, I couldn't. I wanted him to dote on me like he seemed to with everyone else. I would phone his mum and tell her that he cried for her. She told me that when he was with her he cried for me. I found this hard to believe and I dismissed it immediately. When we were getting ready for the day, he would insist on putting his own clothes on and brushing his own teeth. I felt like he didn't want me to do anything for him anymore. Now, I know that children naturally attempt to be as independent as possible at this age. I had learned this during my social work training, although when it came to my own child, I felt that none of this rational explanation applied.

Ethan's mum told me she was going to start doing a night class at a local training college to improve her prospects as a hairdresser. This meant I would be able to have more time with Ethan, but I felt worried that he wouldn't enjoy it.

Given the amount of traveling my new job entailed, every day was completely different and I struggled in adjusting. It seemed that every time I gained a sense of stability, it changed. My work involved emergency response work, something I hadn't done before. I was used to planning my appointment book and following it through until I was finished. If I received an emergency call that warranted my immediate presence, I viewed my day as ruined, but had to do my utmost to hide this when I arrived at where I needed to be. I was perfectly capable of hiding my anguish during working hours.

I was becoming much more irritable and this was showing both at home and at work. I would often come home frustrated that my day hadn't gone as planned and I'd feel like I'd lost complete control of my life. Ethan greeted me with his usual smile, although my face often told the story of how my day at work had been. One evening, I was going to be dropping Ethan home with his mum. She told me she would be home by 7 PM, so I left my mum's at 6:50 to ensure Ethan was home on time. I arrived at 7 PM and she hadn't arrived home yet. Ethan had fallen asleep on the journey and peacefully lay in the back of my car while I was seething with frustration.

It was 7:05 PM and she still hadn't returned home. I had become so dependent on routine that being in any way late would ruin the evening, on top of the day that had also been ruined. She arrived at 7:10 PM and apologized—traffic had been heavy in town and she was delayed getting home. I couldn't accept this and became upset. Unforeseen circumstances were not an excuse in my view and I ensured she knew exactly how I felt. This is how low I had gone. She willingly allowed me to parent Ethan with her and never refused me any opportunities, and this was how I repaid her, by criticizing her for being ten minutes late.

As communication lines were always open, she told my parents what had happened. I am convinced now that this was out of genuine concern, although at the time, I felt she was judging me just like everyone else was. But she knew exactly who I was and exactly what was happening inside my head. Mum and Dad decided to convene a meeting at their house and asked me how I was. They were unaware that I had stopped taking my medication and I told them that my short fuse had to do with work-related stresses that were affecting my mood. I insisted this was the issue and that I would improve in the coming months. Mum had sadness in her eyes, as she knew I was becoming distant. Her adult son was becoming the withdrawn and emotional child that couldn't, despite all his might, forge a meaningful relationship with anyone.

I continued my work, and the morale of my team was high despite the challenging work we had to do. I would discuss my work frustrations openly and everyone supported me. I didn't tell them I had Asperger's although I believe suspicions were growing, especially among the psychiatric nurses. We were all carrying out stressful and demanding work, so my woes were no different than anyone else's. I used to travel to work with a colleague who lived nearby and we had a carpool arrangement. We took turns driving and it was hard not to say too much of what was going on in my home life. As time progressed, we began to trust one another and I was able to communicate more freely. I didn't disclose that I had Asperger's, although I did admit that alterations to my day in the form of emergency calls disrupted me and I found it hard to recover. I felt better getting this off my chest. I was assured that this was normal and would get easier as I gained experience. In my eyes, everyone carried out their duties with dignified grace and character. I found comfort knowing that someone else understood how I felt. I'm sure my face showed exactly how I was feeling. I couldn't keep pretending my feelings were contrary to what my face was showing.

Ethan and I would often go for walks, and by this stage he was no longer using a pram. He often ran ahead of me but would hold my hand if I asked him to. The frustrations and anguish of balancing my work week and hiding my autistic traits were impacting my time with Ethan. When we played outside I would often want to return home to my safe place. I once took Ethan to a play park that was busy and when I saw the amount of people in the area I started to feel uncomfortable. When I was personally approaching three years old, I couldn't manage going to parks as their chaotic nature frightened me. I didn't want Ethan to feel this way and I often took the lead in his play. My mum and first teacher knew I didn't understand the concept of playtime like other children and had to encourage me to participate. I didn't want Ethan to feel this way and offered him guidance throughout his time in the park. I dreaded Ethan standing in the park not knowing what to do so I accompanied him and didn't leave his side. This was the same for every activity we did together. My heart couldn't handle him feeling lost and confused. I never left his side despite the chaotic crowds, and when he wanted to play on his own, I feared that he may be developing the traits I once had. Although he was verbalizing well and demonstrated positive relations with other children, I couldn't stop worrying.

After we left the play park we drove to the beach. As a child I loved the beach and wanted to share my love with Ethan. He enjoyed seeing seagulls and picking up seashells. He sat on a rock and proceeded to take off his shoes to run in the sand. I remember promptly telling him to keep his shoes on and he couldn't understand why. I have particular preferences for surfaces that I walk on and sand is not one of them. It is in an elite club along with trampolines and bouncy castles. Even today I will never walk barefoot on a beach. It's the feeling of not having my entire standing balance that causes me to dislike walking barefoot on sand.

It was approaching summer and Ethan was nearly three years old. His health visitor came to see him and it was clear that he was not demonstrating any traits that would suggest he had any form of autism. He was developing and progressing in line with the developmental milestones and this brought me great comfort. His eating habits and irregular sleep pattern were normal for a child his age and while his mum accepted this, I did not. I still felt Ethan was uncomfortable in my presence and wasn't fond of staying with me. I couldn't imagine him being the same with my parents or his mum. They insisted repeatedly that he was and I shouldn't take Ethan's new habits personally.

Ethan continued to stay with my folks while his mum and I were working weekdays. One evening, Mum called me when I was at work and asked if I would be home in time to see Ethan. (Sometimes my parents left him back with his mum if I wasn't going to be home on time.) I told her that I would be home on time and thought no more of it. It was Friday and a miserable day. The rain battered my windscreen for the duration of the thirty-mile journey home. The weather didn't reflect the summer season. I was looking forward to going home and seeing Ethan. I planned to take him swimming the following day, an activity he looked forward to immensely.

I arrived at my parents' house, took the keys out of my car ignition, and walked through the front door. When I entered Mum was standing in the hallway and the living room door was closed. I could hear

Dad and Ethan behind the door so I knew something was wrong. Mum asked me to come into the kitchen with her and I immediately assumed that someone had died, or something terrible had happened. I walked down our long hallway and entered the kitchen. Mum asked me to sit down; I pulled out a chair from the kitchen table, taking extra care not to score her kitchen floor tiles. I sat down and Mum asked me how I was. I insisted I was fine and that work pressures were affecting me. I could sense Mum saw through this immediately. It was then she told me Ethan had asked her, "Why does Daddy always look so sad?"

CHAPTER 7

I wish I could say that I had an instant moment of clarity. I immediately denied that my mood was poor and insisted that I was feeling the pressures and demands of my work. In truth, I had gained several years' experience at this point and I was able to do my duties quite well. Mum and Dad knew something was wrong, and apparently so did Ethan. My cover was so badly blown that my toddler son could sense that I wasn't the daddy he'd had for the first eighteen months of his life.

Mum suggested I visit the doctor again but I refused. My attitude toward medications triggered my feelings of self-inadequacy. I didn't want to feel broken anymore and I truly believed I could overcome this challenge on my own. I rejected all help and decided I would to try and help myself. Mum sighed and I left the kitchen to go to the living room to see Ethan. I gave Ethan a hug and told him that I would feel better soon.

After Ethan would go to bed or was returned to his mum, I'd spend many hours researching alternative methods to ease my anxieties. I discovered that having a positive hobby or interest could help me. Studies have shown that relaxing hobbies can increase overall well-being. Most people would decide to partake in activities such as yoga, oil painting, attending an exercise class, flower arranging, or stamp collecting. Me? I decided that I wanted to run a marathon. At least, I decided I would give myself time to train to run twenty-six miles. I once thrived at setting myself lofty goals and I believed this could be the answer to everyone's prayers, especially Ethan's.

During one of our Saturday-morning adventures, the two of us went to a sports shop for running gear. I purchased a range of shorts, socks, breathable fabric t-shirts, and shoes. Remember that I hadn't been able to run a single mile to this point, but I was now excited at the thought of running twenty-six miles consecutively. Ethan loved running around the sports shop and he took items off the rails that he thought I needed. The majority of this trip involved telling Ethan to put bikinis, cricket balls, and swimming goggles back where he found them. I spent a fortune on running gear and I was determined to complete this feat of endurance.

I downloaded an app to help me train and I was excited to start. I entered my goal into the app and it calculated a training schedule for me until marathon race day. I told Mum and Dad that I wanted to exercise and explained the benefits it could have on my mood. I believe they were desperate by this point for any change and so they were keen to see this work in making me better again. Mum and Dad also reminded me that such a run would require many hours of training, mostly at Ethan's expense, and I wouldn't see him as often. I had already committed myself and I didn't want to think about this.

I started running short distances with relative ease and adjusted to my running schedule quite well. I loved knowing every training session up until the marathon itself and this gave me comfort. My training had three parts: speed, stamina, and recovery. If I was slower than a previous run I felt defeated despite not being able to run a single mile before I started. Within weeks I was able to comfortably run ten miles and felt ready to embrace the next scheduled challenge. Given my own boundless energy, I was prone to overexertion and injuries. The more I ran, the more I wanted to prove myself to everyone, including Ethan.

For practice, I registered for running events around the country and often asked Mum and Dad to mind Ethan while I ran. It didn't occur to me that I was spending more time away from Ethan as my miles increased. I was regularly running half marathons to build a high level of fitness for the second half of my training program. There were events Mum and Dad would take Ethan to so that he could cheer me on from the sidelines.

I often posed for photographs with my finisher's medal and immediately uploaded them to my social media accounts. I always felt different to everyone else and I was eager for the validation of my peers. I wasn't as open about having Asperger's as I am now and this new and athletic persona suited me so well, I wanted everyone to know about it. I loved getting congratulatory comments, although they only served to boost my own ego, not improve my relationship with Ethan. Ethan was spending so much time with my parents while I was running to show everyone that my life was perfect. In truth, I allowed myself to be consumed by running and by developing this new public character.

I met new people through running and many of them I would still consider friends. An old running partner of mine made an interesting observation. Often, when I would cross the finish line of a half marathon, I would look dejected, even angry. This observation is absolutely right. If the run hadn't gone the way I wanted it to, the run was ruined for me. I would often visualize running the thirteen-mile route and devise my plan of attack. I knew at the starting line when I would stop for water, accelerate, or decelerate.

As running events often take place on public roads and spaces, changes can be made to the running route or the locations of water stations. I once traveled to an eight-mile charity run in Donegal with the intent to break my eight-mile record. I completed my warm-up and my pre-race ritual of visualizing every step I would take on the route.

Before the run began, the race director commanded everyone's attention, announcing that a portion of the route had to be altered due to a traffic collision between miles four and five. I felt so ill prepared after this news and I couldn't cope with the change. I set off, but after only two miles I pulled out of the race and went home.

I was to take Ethan for lunch when I got home and I entered my parents' house dejected. I told them I had hurt my knee and couldn't finish the race. Ethan and I went for lunch and I couldn't hide my frustration from him. He ate his lunch slowly and I didn't eat mine at all. I just sat there staring at my food. He quickly told me that I have to eat my lunch to grow up to be big and strong. Sitting across from him, a sobering realization came to light. I wasn't running for my fitness, nor was I running to improve my health or well-being. I was running to hide who I was again. Social media is the main platform for demonstrating one's life, and the life I wanted to show was that of a competent, athletic, doting father. In real life, outside of the social media newsfeeds I carefully curated, I was none of these things.

I realized I couldn't simply stop, though, and that I had to see this challenge through to the end. I had set myself a goal and I was going to do everything to achieve it despite the consequence of spending less time with Ethan. I was well beyond the halfway point and my miles on the road had to increase beyond the thirteen I was used to running. I had to edge closer to twenty miles.

I was still working far from home and I often returned home to run. Some of the training days on my schedule coincided with my days with Ethan and I asked Mum and Dad to mind Ethan on my weekend days so I could complete my longer runs. I ran the length and breadth of the country in the rain and hail. I couldn't allow anyone to see that I was anything other than committed to my goals. I fear that if I stopped now I'd blow my cover once again.

My training and running continued and I received many medals, albeit only finisher medals. Luckily I wasn't far gone enough to actually believe I could win the marathon I was set to run. The final eight weeks saw my miles increase dramatically. Ethan would ask me if he was going to see his grandparents and I'd confirm. He knew I enjoyed running and that I was taking it very seriously. Mum and Dad often reminded me that my time with Ethan should be precious and leaving him to go running was unfair to him. I reassured them that I was so close to my goal and that I only had weeks left until marathon day.

My long runs were between eighteen and twenty miles—my body could feel the strain. I planned to run a nineteen-mile training route that had a three-mile incline. The route offered a spectacular view of the city from the hillside and I looked forward to the challenge. I had bought the custom shoes I would run the marathon in and I was preparing to run in them for my longest run yet. I had just two weeks of training left; my nineteen and twenty-two mile runs would complete my training schedule. I would run them on consecutive Sunday mornings when Ethan was with his mum.

I woke at 7 AM to complete my nineteen-mile run and drove to the starting line I had chosen. At night I would obsess about my marathon pace and wanted to complete the twenty-six-mile course in five hours. I set off toward the mountain I had to run up and played my music through my earphones as I ran. My marathon shoes softened the constant blows of my large legs smashing against the pavement and I felt great. I had reached the foot of the mountain when a stabbing pain in my right hip rendered me immobile. A reasonable plan of action would have been to walk back to the car, rest at home, and attempt the run next week. But back then, I wasn't a reasonable man. I limped rigidly to the top of the mountain, taking care not to over flex my stricken hip. At mile thirteen I couldn't continue. I was so annoyed with myself and felt the previous months of training had been in vain. I pulled up beside a nearby farm and sat on the ground for a ten-minute break. I tried to come to terms with this sudden change to my run and I closed my eyes to focus. All I could think about was how disappointed I was— I couldn't regain my composure. I kept thinking about Ethan and that I couldn't stop running, certainly not now when I was so close to achieving what I had set out to do. I was just starting to realize how much time I'd spent away from Ethan.

As I sat on the ground overlooking the city, a car stopped beside me and offered to take me back to my starting position. On marathon day, failure wasn't an option and I politely declined. I hoisted myself to my feet and limped the long and painful six miles to my car. I marvel now at the physical and emotional pain I would subject myself to in order to prove myself.

I thought running would make me happy and a better parent, but as I reflect back on this time, I recognize that my attitude was wrong and that I may have started running for the wrong reasons, mainly for self-validation. I ran believing I could mold myself into someone Ethan would be proud of and to lift my low mood. I ran obsessively and aimlessly while chasing an idea of perfection, an ideal I created in my own mind.

Later, Ethan inquired as to why I was walking strangely, I told him I had hurt myself running and he kissed my leg better. He gave me a hug and asked me if I was happy and I told him I was. How could I explain myself to a child and expect him to understand?

My dad recommended I see a physical therapist to assess the damage of my right hip. I arrived at the therapist's office and he quickly diagnosed a torn right hip flexor muscle. He told me I couldn't run the marathon due to the high risk of permanent damage. I didn't agree with him and limped back out to my car. Let's be honest; there was no hope of me not turning up at the start line on marathon day. I decided I'd walk the twenty miles I had left for my training the following week and rest until marathon day.

I could feel the tearing and cracking of my hip as I walked my final twenty miles of training. I came home and collapsed on my living room floor. My right leg had locked completely and I crawled to my sofa to set up camp. I had completed my training program and couldn't believe I had come this far. A tapering period is recommended in the final two or three weeks of any marathon training program, although I decided I would rest instead. I was taking anti-inflammatory medication to ease the hip pain as well as using topical gel. Ethan loved adventuring and I often hobbled slowly behind him as he ran free. I was in terrible pain but refused to seek any medical attention or return to the physical therapist.

One week before the marathon, Ethan and I returned to the beach. He loved running on the sand, petting passing dogs, and he ran so far ahead of me that I couldn't catch him. He turned to see his sore and anguished daddy standing helplessly some distance away; I couldn't walk any farther. He walked slowly back to me and told me to take him home because he knew I wasn't fit for his fun and games. I was only too happy to oblige. I brought Ethan to my parent's house and discussed my race day plans with them. For the marathon, the main spectator points were from mile twenty onward and I told them to have Ethan ready to see me running by. Mum and Dad urged me not to participate and I insisted that I felt well enough to complete the course.

The day before race day had finally arrived and I took Ethan over to collect my race pack. It included my race number, T-shirt, and race day instructions. It was one of the warmest weeks on record and it was explained at the race briefing that the course had a minor alteration. My plan was kaput! I went home upset that the route I had studied for so long had changed the day before the race. Not completing the marathon was out of the question, though. I took Ethan over to my mum's house and showed them my race pack. Everyone knew I was running the course and I couldn't back out now. I would have been a disappointment to everyone, or so I thought.

My hip pain had eased slightly with rest, but I knew I still wasn't fit to run twenty-six miles. I went to bed worried that I wouldn't make it; I couldn't allow that to happen. I stretched lightly and opened my bedroom window to look at the running route I would be completing in the morning. The authorities were placing traffic cones at the side of the road in preparation for the event and my nerves started to build. I tossed and turned most of the night because of the pain and anxiety and before I knew it, it was time for breakfast.

I knew I couldn't let anyone down so I forced myself to eat, took my pain medication, and packed some to take with me for during the race. I arrived at the start line along with the many thousands who would be running with me. I walked uncomfortably amongst the sea of people and realized the magnitude of what I was about to do. I didn't know many people as I wasn't with a running club and often ran alone. I refused to have any photographs taken by the race photographers and I nervously took my position behind the starting line. The starting line had a festival atmosphere and the noise was starting to rattle me. As I stood amongst the runners, the chants, cheers, whistles, and music amalgamated into the insufferable auditory hell that frightened me so much. My common reflex returned as my hands lifted up toward my ears, and I closed my eyes to regain my composure. I managed to block out the noise of the crowds until the boom of the starter pistol brought the race to life. We all ran for our lives amidst the screams and cheers. I heard several people call my name but I couldn't place them in the crowds. I looked at my watch as I ran and the 8:45 AM temperature was 68 degrees Fahrenheit. The adrenaline helped me run comfortably up to the halfway point.

The temperature continued to rise and I could feel my legs getting heavier and heavier. The masses around me had thinned as all my fellow runners were fit for the run. I, in my foolish determination, had decided not to stay at home. The heat started to halt runners in their tracks and most began to walk to ensure dehydration didn't set in. I saw my dad and Ethan at mile sixteen where the route passed by the front of my house. By that stage, I was limping badly, and Ethan clapped his hands in support of me. At mile nineteen a young girl collapsed in front of me as we jogged toward the final stages of the race. Some fellow runners and I gathered around her until the paramedics came to assess her; she was in a bad way. We were told to proceed to the finish line as we couldn't obstruct the ambulance reaching the fallen runner.

Given the soaring temperatures, water sprinklers were positioned along the route to bring our body temperatures down. Up until mile twenty I hadn't taken advantage of the sprinklers since I didn't like wearing wet clothes that could restrict my movement. I was starting to feel faint, though, and decided I had to go under the sprinkler to reduce the risk of overheating and suffering the same fate as the girl. As the icy mist connected with me, my entire body contracted and the stabbing pain in my hip flared up worse than it had ever been. I cried out in pain and basically hopped along for the next two miles with my damp clothes clinging to my body. I was finally nearing the end of the route. I had suffered so much pain during the race that I realized I had already passed the route change that had terrified me only a day before.

By mile twenty-three, I was completely reduced to a weakened hobbled pace, and a volunteer first-aider urged me to stop. As I shambled onward, she kept alongside me on her bicycle and gave me an additional bottle of water to drink or pour over my head. I took the emergency pain relief I had in my pocket, determined to finish.

Mile twenty-five brought the sternest challenge, a two-hundred-meter incline toward the finish line. As I approached the hill, I saw Ethan run out onto the road. He came up to me and gave me a hug in the middle of the road. My mum captured the wonderful moment on camera. After this, my parents quickly took Ethan up ahead to the finishing line so they could watch me make my big finish.

As I hobbled to the twenty-six mile marker, I checked my watch and noted that five hours and fifty minutes had passed. I was fifty minutes over my expected finishing time. Mum, Dad, Ethan, and my closest friends had assembled at the finish line to see my triumphant crossing. As I turned the corner toward the finish line I decided to run. I knew the press and television cameras were present so I had to put on a good show. As my friends saw me cross the finish line, none knew about the challenges I had faced leading up to that point.

The giant finisher's medal was placed around my neck and the weight of it nearly caused me to fall flat on my face. I embraced Ethan and told him what I had accomplished. He replied by asking me to buy him an ice cream cone. How could I say no?

Mum took him home later and I went off to share a meal with my friends to celebrate. As the adrenaline from the race stated to fade, I was reduced to crippling pain and excused myself early to go home. I remember crawling up my steep and narrow staircase to bed and removing my marathon clothing before falling into bed. I realized I wasn't as elated as I should have been. I shared my triumph on social media and received numerous congratulations from all I knew. The new persona I had hand carved was complete. I appeared to be a strong man in the prime of his life, exactly what I wanted.

As I lay in bed, many fleeting thoughts came and went from my restless mind. One question immediately came to mind: Had it all been worth it? I had started running to make my son proud, but his main concern on marathon day was where the ice cream man was situated. I was likening his feelings/reaction toward me to those of an adult. I didn't realize at the time that he processed information in his own childlike way. Here I was, at the end of my spiritual marathon journey, and I did feel proud that I managed to run the twenty-six miles, but I had channeled so much energy into gaining approval that I had subjected myself to horrific pain and obsession.

The following day I went to the beach with Emily and her infant son. I walked straight to the water's edge and sat in the surf. It was a warm day and the cold salt water soothed my torn muscles. My hip was in incredible pain and I can safely say that I wasn't good company that day. Emily asked why I wasn't feeling elated at the fact that I achieved such a feat. The answer (although not spoken to her) was the stark realization that I had missed so much of Ethan's second year. Instead of elation at having run twenty-six miles, all I was left with was regret. When he had run onto the road to greet me during the marathon, I saw how tall he had become. I ran the hills and valleys alone and I used running to isolate myself from everyone. Having an upcoming event was the perfect excuse not to socialize with friends and I saw little of them, although they did support and encourage me during my training.

After the marathon, I hung up my running shoes and decided to take a break. I felt a profound sense of regret that I had missed so much time with Ethan. Anytime I looked at my medal hanging up on my bedroom wall, my pride was overshadowed with guilt. It upset me greatly. The time spent running in the rain would have been better spent in warmth with Ethan. I know now that I hadn't eradicated my demons. The feeling of deep connection that I longed for with Ethan hadn't returned, nor did I feel enough affection coming from him. It wasn't his fault. I couldn't possibly have built a relationship with him given the amount of time I ran away from him, literally!

Some time after the marathon, Mum and Dad convened yet another meeting with me to discuss how I was. They first congratulated me and told me how proud they were that I had the determination to run a marathon. I was happy to hear this praise from them; it meant a lot—I felt pleased that I had been able to persevere when the road didn't have an end in sight and that I'd faced the challenge head-on. But I also heard a "but" in their approval coming and braced myself.

Mum brought up the fact that while my feat was impressive, it had come at the expense of missing most of Ethan's second year. While this was extremely uncomfortable to hear, I tried to justify my running life as a means to improve my mood and overall well-being. Mum and Dad correctly pointed out that I had simply replaced one issue with another. My task should have been to improve my relationship with Ethan. I couldn't disagree with them on any of this.

My mood was generally better when I was running, my sleeping pattern vastly improved, and I lost weight. I felt happy in my own skin and liked wearing smaller clothing sizes. I had read that running released endorphins and I had chased the endorphin-fuelled euphoria every time I laced up my running shoes and charged head-on through the challenge. I had temporarily improved my mood, although my deep psychological issues still lay dormant in my mind. I had turned a healthy and fun pastime into yet another toxic obsession. This was no different than any other life pursuit I had worked toward and accomplished previously. My pride was such that I couldn't feel for one second that I was different from anyone else. Anytime I strayed too far from the pack, I worked tirelessly to fit back in.

I still wasn't interested in embracing and accepting who I was. I finally had to admit to myself, and my parents, that I had chosen to sacrifice time with my son just so I could appear to be like every other parent in the world. I wanted to be Ethan's hero. The fact that my brain told me to go about this in the way that I did horrified me. My fight-or-flight response had been triggered and I had chosen flight. When I was at school, my response was always to fight but I had become much gentler in adulthood. I wasn't physically aggressive anymore but I still avoided conflict or disagreement at all costs.

Looking back, I thought I was running from all my problems—I thought if I ran long enough they would stop chasing me and leave me alone. Although I had found a way of releasing energy and focusing my mind, I had paid a hefty price. I seldom saw Ethan or my parents. My friends had stopped inviting me to social outings, as they knew I was rigidly sticking to my training schedule. I had severed all of my meaningful connections in order to show the world I was happy.

Ethan asking my parents why I looked so sad haunted me still and I had come to a fork in the road. It was now time to decide what direction the rest of my life would take. I couldn't continue creating public images of myself for the rest of my life. These futile attempts often caused me stress that couldn't be hidden from Ethan, and my family was withdrawing from me too. I simply refused to listen to any of their advice and I only pursued the options that felt most comfortable to me. All I wanted was to bring some order and clarity to my life. The second path would be the dark and misty path I often refused to go down, the path to accepting I had Asperger's and coming to terms with it.

When I arrived at this emotional fork in the road, I realized that I always went down the path that was familiar to me. Although this was a path well traveled, it always had negative consequences and eventually led me back to where I had started. I had repeatedly made this decision throughout my life when things were difficult, and I couldn't continue the impossible task of using this coping method to hide who I was.

After the talk with my parents, I found myself home alone, while Ethan was back with his mum. I lay down on his tiny bed, my feet extending far beyond the bottom of his mattress, and held his teddy bear to my chest. As I stared at his colorful posters around the room a thought occurred to me. I could never remember Mum and Dad being sad throughout my childhood. They accepted and loved me for who I was. When Mum talked about my upbringing, she did so with a smile. They knew I wasn't like the other children in my playgroups or school. They never doubted me nor did they give up on me. They fought so courageously for me and defended me. I decided that I owed it to them and to Ethan to try and heal. I decided I no longer wished to be ashamed of myself.

I knew I had to change direction and make positive changes. I wasn't foolish enough to believe I could rid myself of Asperger's, although I needed to attempt alternative treatments to help me live with it and feel at peace within myself. Running a marathon was one challenge—this was epic in comparison. I decided I would take the first step and contact my doctor to arrange an appointment for as soon as possible.

The first step in most recovery programs is admitting and acknowledging the problem. I always viewed having Asperger's as the problem. It wasn't. The real problem was my inability to live with it—to accept it as a part of me. My life was based on denial, dishonesty, and obsession. The previous year had flown by for me and I couldn't allow my obsessions to take any more time out of Ethan's upbringing.

A few days later it was time to see my doctor again. I requested the day off work and rehearsed what I would say during the appointment. I sat in the waiting room staring at my shoes knowing this would be the hardest journey I would ever have to go on, but I had to do it for my son. The doctor called my name and welcomed me back. I admitted to him that I had stopped taking my medication and had experienced a downward spiral since. I explained my obsessional traits had returned and this had impacted my relationships with my family, friends, and Ethan. I then told him about how I had taken up running and had completed a marathon. The doctor enlightened me that while exercise is crucial to a healthy lifestyle, my obsessive tendencies had taken over and now outweighed the health benefits. In fact my obsession had stopped me from resting to heal from physical injuries, and my faltering relationships with the people most important to me lowered my mood faster than running ever improved it. The doctor recommended an immediate return to my medication, psychological therapy, and cognitive behavioral therapy. With a deep breath, I gave my consent and he promised to send referral letters that afternoon.

I later collected my medication from the pharmacy and I was pleased that I had finally accepted advice that would benefit me. I felt so positive that I immediately shared with my parents that I actually had taken advice from another human being! They were delighted and told me I had made the right decision. It must have been a very difficult year for them to watch me take such a sudden deterioration after having several years of progress. What a relief it must have been for them to hear this news.

Ethan came to stay with me that evening and he was happy to be back. We decided to go to a nearby funfair as it was a warm evening. Ethan was so excited. We sat on a bench within the funfair and watched the world go by; Ethan was occupied with a balloon and ice cream. He laughed, smiled, and seemed to enjoy my company. He wanted to go on the Ferris wheel and I happily obliged. As the ride reached the top of its rotation I saw the city lights spread out below. The bright orange color reminded me of a scorched earth, one that I had created throughout my life. I came to the sobering realization that I had alienated everybody.

CHAPTER 8

Having gone to see the doctor, I knew that it would be some weeks before the appointment letters for my therapies would arrive. Until then, I made the promise to my parents and Ethan that I would take my medication every morning, and I reinstated the task in my daily routine. Now that I had stopped running, I was spending more time with Ethan and I discovered how independent he had become during my absence—he was able to use the toilet and wash himself in the shower. The more one-on-one time I spent with Ethan, the more I sadly came to the realization that I should have been the one who taught him these new abilities.

Like almost everything in the past two years, autumn crept up on me and caught me by surprise. Ethan and I went for walks to admire the fall colors and he enjoyed picking up the leaves so I could tell him which tree they had fallen from. I bought him Wellington boots and he joyfully ran through puddles and mud to my disdain. I was trying to spend quality time with Ethan on his terms, although I often tried to stop him from doing things that I wasn't comfortable with. I stayed with him constantly and I didn't allow him the space I should have. As I've shared, walking on different textures was a no-go for me. I felt I had to warn Ethan of the horrors of walking on uneven ground.

Ethan and I have our own duties within our household to ensure that it runs like a well-oiled machine. I would make meals, wash our clothes, and meet our transportation requirements. One of Ethan's duties was to bring me letters that were sitting on the porch. I taught him how to filter the mail; takeout menus and telephone directories were placed immediately in the bin and letters with my name on them were presented to me. One day, Ethan gave me a letter that clearly wasn't a bill and I was curious to see what it was. As I opened the letter, Ethan sat beside me, eager to see who had written. It had finally arrived; it was an appointment letter to attend psychological therapy.

I just sat there and stared at the appointment date and location—when consenting to the referral, there was one major detail I hadn't considered. Given my professional position, I often had clients attend the same therapies in the same location, and the therapist would most likely know me. When working as a community social worker, I entered the building with my proud and charismatic persona. I didn't want to sacrifice this "illusion" by entering as a patient. I didn't want to risk my cover being blown yet again or have anyone see me as anything other than the man I projected myself to be.

I decided that I couldn't risk professional compromise, so I called the number on the appointment letter a few days later and told them I didn't wish to attend any longer and that my appointment should be offered to someone else. I was relieved at first until it hit me that I was running yet again. I was hiding away from the experts who could help me face the truth. Ethan returned to me that night from his mum's house and I felt that I had failed him again by canceling my appointment. I knew that Ethan could sense my sadness to the point that I felt he didn't want to be with me anymore. When he came to my house, he cried at the doorstep and he didn't want to come in. He eventually settled with a large dose of the finest childhood cure, ice cream. As he sat beside me eating his ice cream in silence, I finally admitted to myself that I had made a huge mistake. I was running away from the path less traveled toward the familiar yet destructive one.

When Monday morning came, I was back at work and dealing with a very complex case that demanded my immediate presence. I often have district nurses, doctors, and care agencies contact me throughout the day and that day was no different. I felt my phone ring in the middle of my visit and I asked the client if I could be excused to my car to take the call. When I answered the call it was a therapist within the psychological support service and he introduced himself to me. For this story, I will call him Michael. He called to confirm if I was choosing to decline the therapy for which I had been referred. I asked if my appointment was still available and Michael confirmed that it was. He then asked if I had any concerns that immediately caused me to panic and decline the appointment. I immediately opened up, which was completely out of the ordinary. I told him of my professional position and that I didn't wish to be compromised. I was immediately given reassurance; the referral letter requested my case was treated with sensitivity given my occupation. Michael informed me that he specialized in treating adults with Asperger's and other forms of autism. I was delighted to hear this and went about the rest of my day feeling lucky to get this second chance at an appointment.

When I got home that night, I called my parents to inform them of what had transpired over the past few days. Instead of being disappointed or even scolding, they were proud that I was finally accepting help and acknowledged that it was a huge step in the right direction for me. By accepting the appointment, I felt a larger sense of pride than I had when completing the marathon only a few months before. I didn't look forward to the appointment, but I knew I had to go through with it. The appointment was scheduled for the following week and I remember dreading it more than anything I can remember. I had a misconceived belief that therapy was all about being emotionally undressed, examined, and judged.

As the therapist worked the same hours as me, I had another decision to face: Do I tell my line manager the truth or do I simply request the time off work with no further comment? The decision was incredibly difficult and I would love to write about how I suddenly decided to open up and tell my boss who I really was; unfortunately, my therapy hadn't started yet and I chose the latter option. I just couldn't bring myself to remove the smokescreen just yet. I was managing reasonably well at work because I had adopted a task-based approach: I wrote what I had to do that day and went home at the end. I still struggled with crisis intervention, though, and often went home annoyed if my days didn't follow the plan I set at the start of the day.

Taking my medication every morning gave me a sense of comfort, and with each passing tablet I was taking a positive step toward living with Asperger's. Even after just a few weeks, I noticed my appetite increased and my sleeping pattern was returning to how it had been when I was emotionally well. It normally takes approximately two months for the medication to have a full effect, and any form of waiting or queuing can usually cause me distress, but I was happy to wait knowing I would eventually feel better. Taking the medication wasn't easy by any means; the large capsule was as difficult to swallow as my pride.

The morning of my initial appointment came and I had the sudden urge not to go. I decided not to eat any breakfast as I was unsure my nerves would allow me to keep it down. The day had come where I would have to walk into a familiar building, not as a professional but as a client who desperately needed help. I brought my pen and notebook with me to act as a shield. I often held my books close to my chest like an iron breastplate. It was a habit I only realized I had when I entered the building to wait for my appointment. I checked in at the appointment desk and sat in the waiting room nervously. It occurred to me as

I waited that I could still flee. All I had to do was stand up, take my car keys out of my pocket, exit the building, and drive away.

I had made my decision—it was red alert and time to leave. I stooped and gathered my diary and other belongings, and was about to leave the waiting room when Michael came down the corridor toward me. He welcomed me, introduced himself, and thanked me for coming to the appointment. I accepted his firm handshake and didn't admit that he had caught me trying to escape. I followed him down the corridor to the therapy suite, much in the way a condemned man would approach the electric chair. I found it very difficult to deepen my shallow breathing and I resisted the urge to turn and run.

I imagined an overly clinical setting, where I would lie on a chaise longue and discuss my deepest and darkest secrets while the therapist smoked a pipe and took copious notes. The room turned out to have a large east-facing window with a similar view of the river to the one from my bedroom window. I'm immediately drawn to windows and always give in to the urge to walk up to them to take in their particular view. This time was no different as I walked past facing sofas to admire the view. Michael stood beside me and asked me if I knew the reason I was seeing him. Still in full character, I joked that I had heard he had a nice window that I could look out of.

Michael stood at the window with me and explained that he was a psychological therapist who had worked for many years as a specialist nurse with those with autism and related disorders. He informed me that he also had worked with numerous professionals in similar positions as me, achieving positive outcomes with them. It takes a lot to distract me from a scenic view, but this point immediately focused my attention on him and not the storm clouds gathering in the east. He asked if I was shocked by what he had just said and I told him that I certainly was. Up until that point, I felt like a confidence trickster who had developed a certain charisma that helped me get to where I was. I had developed a successful career and bought my own house, all while keeping my autism at bay.

I was given an outline of what my therapy would look like and this went a long way in keeping me interested. The psychological therapy would help me to understand the particular circumstances that exacerbated my autistic traits. Past events and circumstances were shaping my thinking and behavior in the present and I would be facing those issues, not ignoring them and running away. The psychological therapy would identify the triggers that influenced my behavior and the cognitive behavioral therapy would, in theory, provide me with new coping mechanisms.

In what seemed very little time, my session was completed and Michael gave me a task to complete before my next appointment. I received an instruction to write about my earliest memories of school—any specific examples of interactions that upset me or made me angry. I joked that he would require an entire week to hear about each individual incident and he insisted that he didn't. He told me to see if there were any connections between the individual incidents and if any patterns emerged. He explained that my second appointment would be in three weeks because that additional time would be needed to recall all my childhood memories into a notepad and fully reflect on them.

I bought a fresh notepad to write my deepest, darkest thoughts in. I had never kept a journal nor had I ever been keen to join Anne Frank, Virginia Woolf, or "a wimpy kid" in the club of elite diarists. I brought my notepad and pen everywhere with me, and wrote down everything that came to mind when thinking about my earliest days. Ethan always inquired as to why I was writing all the time and I told him I was writing Santa to tell him how good his behavior was.

I was sitting with Ethan at the kitchen table one day when a memory came to mind. I remembered my first playgroup and staring out our living room window after my mum was told my needs could not be met there. I closed my eyes and pictured the view from that window as a three-year-old. I tried to visualize the view through the distortion caused by the rain trickling down the window. I just stood there and stared into the distance, unable to speak or understand why I wasn't allowed to return to the cars I had left behind. It made me think about how far I had come in the space of twenty-three years. I immediately wrote this down and returned to drawing pictures with Ethan.

All the way through primary school I couldn't integrate with other children. I often stared helplessly on as the other children played and got to know one another. I didn't understand them and they didn't understand me. Sometimes my teachers had to send me back to the classroom if I became too aggressive on the playground. I regularly would watch the other children playing from the classroom window, longing to be like them.

One day while we were at the park, a little boy about Ethan's age approached him while he was playing with his toy cars. Ethan was happy that another child spoke to him and was keen to play. I left my park bench with my notepad and pen in hand to be close to Ethan— I wasn't sure how he would react to someone wanting to play with his cars. I stood over the two children and my towering stature obviously unnerved the other little boy who only wanted to play with Ethan. I had wanted to be on hand to help Ethan play, much in the same way I had wanted someone to help me when I was his age. Instead I ruined this playtime encounter for him as the other boy ran off.

Even at work, I always kept my notepad and pen with me, forever writing down notes from my fleeting childhood memories. My colleagues often asked what I was doing and this would have been the perfect chance to open up to them. I had been working there for two years by this point and I knew my colleagues extremely well, yet I still didn't want to reveal the true me. I even brought my notepad and pen into our staff room; the only place I didn't write was in my shower.

During all this, I suddenly decided that I wanted to sell and move to a new house. I shared the idea with Ethan, but he adored his room and was very hesitant to part company with the space we had made our own. I, on the other hand, had already decided that I wanted a larger home than what our modest two-bedroom home offered us. I told my parents and Ethan's mum of my decision, although nobody wanted me to undergo any unnecessary stress. They all believed the home we had made for ourselves was appropriate and warned me that having a sudden change of scenery at this point in my life was not the best idea. In other words, they were trying to tell me to help myself first before making any more major life decisions. I thanked them for their input, considered their thoughts for several minutes, then I decided to put my house on the market.

Ethan and I started house hunting again and found the ideal home. It was recently renovated and complete with a new kitchen, a new bathroom, and nice tiling throughout the hallway. The upstairs bedroom window that I'd take for myself offered a perfect view. In fact, it had a much nicer view than my old bedroom given the higher altitude. From this new bedroom window I could see the local football stadium, the home of my beloved Derry City Football Club. During a second viewing of the house, another memory came to mind, so I started to write it in my notepad. In this particular memory, I remembered playing a football match at school where I clearly wasn't performing well. My physical education teacher decided to make a halftime substitution and pulled me from the game—I was livid. I was foul, abusive, and stormed off the pitch with my football boots still on my feet. I fled up the staircase next to our changing room into an empty classroom. I stood at the window and watched the rest of the match as my team lost. I eventually returned to the locker room to change into my school uniform and I was met by an impenetrable wall of silence from my team. My classmates scurried out of the changing room and my PE teacher asked to speak to me. I was quick to inform him that my team had lacked aerial presence in the second half and that it cost my teammates the match. My teacher responded to this remark by telling me that my terrifying exit from the pitch had frightened everyone present, including himself. I remember feeling a sense of guilt upon learning that I had scared and intimidated my entire team, not to mention my coach.

I left my second viewing of the house knowing that I wanted it and made an offer. In the meantime, someone agreed to buy my house at a price much greater than my asking price! I couldn't believe my luck and neither could my parents.

It was two weeks since my first therapy session and Michael called me to confirm my appointment for the following week. He questioned whether I had noticed any patterns or correlation within my writing and I told him I hadn't. Later, with Ethan present, I reviewed my notes trying to find a link of some kind. When I found it, I was surprised. In most of my childhood memories I was alone, staring out windows.

My second therapy appointment came and I confidently went straight to the therapy room to find Michael standing by the window. I entered and sat down on the facing sofas with my notepad and pen. Without exchanging pleasantries, I immediately started to share with him that most of my sad memories from childhood involved staring out windows. I asked if this was an appropriate link since I couldn't find any others. We discussed the memories I had written down—all involving me standing by a window alone—and Michael explained that staring into space or out windows was a common autistic trait. In my case it created two conflicting emotions: one being the feeling of being marginalized, the other being a feeling of security. I was staring out at a world I didn't feel a part of, hiding behind the safety of the glass. This was quite a revelation to me. I associated the glass barrier between me and the world with safety. Michael asked me to speak more explicitly about my behaviors as a child and I found this difficult. I explained that I would often scare other children because they didn't understand me. I explained that I couldn't verbalize well and I was often isolated because of this. He asked if I felt that people understood me now as a grown man. I explained that I had adapted and become an expert in making people believe I was something that I wasn't, but that over time I feared people would see the frightened and insecure person I truly was. Michael reassured that "autistic masking" was extremely common and confirmed that this was exactly what I was doing. This had been incredibly difficult to admit to him, but I felt an immediate sense of relief once I accepted and acknowledged my longtime behavior.

Michael told me that my sessions would be weekly from now until the end of my four-week treatment. My task for the next session was to document my obsessional behaviors from every stage of my life. One of those obsessions turned out to be my interest in space. I had even started blogging about the universe over the years. I was also fascinated with the *Titanic* and I still know where most of the passenger amenities were situated on the ship. At my next therapy session I listed out my obsessions and Michael asked me to talk about them. For the entire session, I discussed everything from galaxy clusters to *Titanic*'s steam engine assembly. When discussing the condition of *Titanic*'s wreck, Michael interrupted me to tell me that our session was over and I had spoken the entire session without allowing him to have any input. He told me that despite him looking away or staring at his watch, I didn't stop talking. The clear lesson from the second session was that I wasn't allowing others to speak or have a point of view. He told me to reflect on how many meaningful interactions I had lost due to my incessant and obsessional conversation style.

I thought about what Michael had said at the end of our session at home that night and came to the conclusion that his observations were entirely true. I couldn't form a meaningful or healthy relationship with anyone because I had to steer the conversation in my favor to feel like I was fitting in, while in reality, this desire to fit in distanced me more from those people I wanted in my life. I acknowledged that I had to try to interpret when a conversation was becoming one-sided, to try and make deeper connections with people.

Our next session focused on my social difficulties. Social situations were still very difficult for me and I explained my internal pain when a situation caused me to panic. I shared my social anxieties and how my hands would automatically cover my ears if I became overwhelmed. Michael asked if I had been to a concert before and I confirmed that I had. I explained that concert noise was organized and that the crowd was all there for one purpose, to see the live act. It is not chaotic nor is it disorganized enough to cause me to panic. He pointed out that every-one who attended Ethan's birthday party had been there for the same purpose, but clearly my mind didn't allow me to think that way. This was another huge revelation and I was enjoying learning more about the mechanics of autism and myself.

When Ethan came to stay with me the next time, we were preparing to move out of our house. He helped me pack boxes and told me that he was excited to see his new bedroom. I asked Ethan if he wanted to build a fort out of the boxes and he was delighted. I immediately got to work on constructing our fort and I had all the boxes ready to start the project. I was going to build our fort in the living room until Ethan asked if the fort could be built in his bedroom. I had planned the fort well and believed my location to be the wiser option, but I saw Ethan's face and recalled what I had learned in my therapy session: to allow others to contribute and help. I promptly moved all the boxes to his room and we started to build the fort together. Once completed, we sat inside our fort on Ethan's bedroom floor and he came over to give me a hug. It was his last night in our first house and seeing Ethan smile lifted my spirits.

We moved into our new home the following week. We were just in time for Christmas and we immediately put our Christmas decorations around the house. I allowed Ethan to help me decorate the Christmas tree, despite having a strong idea of what I wanted it to look like. It was the first time that I felt like I was letting go, although this was short-lived as I rearranged the tree again after he went to bed. We had such a nice Christmas that year; I noticed improvements in myself and displayed a higher level of self-awareness. I noticed Ethan was becoming much happier in my company and luckily he didn't realize that I had altered the tree he had designed.

My final two therapy sessions resumed after Christmas and it was time to face some hard truths. Michael commended me on my compliance with the therapy and that our mutually agreed upon goal of finding reasons for my behaviors was almost accomplished. He established that my sense of order was now becoming slightly more negotiable and that I was allowing others in. I told him about my relationship with Ethan and his perception that I always looked sad. The reason I looked so sad was because I couldn't allow my sense of order or my false character to be compromised.

Michael asked if I had known what Asperger's syndrome was when I was four years old, and I confirmed that I hadn't. He told me that Ethan would not understand what it was either and that he would not judge me, much in the same way I wouldn't judge him. I discussed my fear that Ethan would grow into adulthood resenting me—in the same way I resented myself. I was subconsciously restricting and "protecting" Ethan and not allowing him to find his own way. After learning what my parents and I know now about autism, it was very clear that by age three, I was demonstrating obvious Asperger tendencies, from not being able to verbalize to the repetitive behaviors I adopted. Ethan was always the opposite and had varied interests.

The difficult discussion of the pregnancy journey came up in our penultimate session. Michael and I identified that the sudden change in my circumstances and not knowing what the future held caused me to regress to a debilitating lack of functioning. I couldn't come to terms with Ethan's arrival and I attempted to control the situation to ease my own mind, without regard for anyone else. Throughout my adolescence and early adulthood, I avoided conflict and disagreements. I would often agree with someone to avoid any form of confrontation since I couldn't emotionally cope with such a scenario. I agreed with Michael's evaluation that the factors of avoiding conflict and the pregnancy had made me become much more sensitive over the years.

It was finally time for my last session and Michael wrote a detailed report that would be sent to the cognitive behavioral therapist. The conclusions were that I had a strong negative bias, a loss of identity due to masking my condition from those around me, and obsessional patterns of behavior that impacted my interactions and relationships. Although some of the points documented on the report were difficult to read, I was happy to see that it highlighted my growing acceptance of my condition and willingness to receive help.

I read the report and agreed with everything that was stated. It had been very difficult discussing my feelings, but I had persevered and opened up throughout the sessions. Michael informed me that we needed to identify what areas to focus on when the time came to commence with cognitive behavioral therapy (CBT). I was informed that this could take some time given the waiting list that existed for the service. I never thought about my childhood as much as I did during those eight weeks I waited to start CBT. I hadn't realized that my issues during childhood impacted my emotional growth as an adult, and I had genuinely believed that I was constantly overcoming challenges. The truth was I was never overcoming any challenges, only shelving them until they reappeared at a later date.

I certainly would have been able to cope better in life if I had availed of therapy earlier. Instead my emotions were misdirected and I believed I was emotionally stronger if I wasn't taking medications or attending therapy. I feared being analyzed and so retreated to the safety of my glass box. Trying to keep up appearances over the many years had become so exhausting that I often retreated to the safe place I had created in my mind.

Mum and Dad were delighted that I had finished my therapy and that my medication was starting to take effect. When at work, I no longer planned out my days nor did I panic when a crisis situation came to my attention. It still made me feel slightly uneasy, but it certainly didn't ruin my day as it once did. When growing up, I always wondered and worried why I was so different from everyone else, and for the first time in my life, I finally had comfort in knowing why I was the way I am. I just wish I'd had the answers much earlier in life—especially before Ethan was born.

My therapy made me fully realize how much my parents had done for me (and still do to this day). It would have been so easy for them to allow me to go my own way when I entered adulthood. Without my parents helping me to have some moments of clarity along the way, I don't know where I would have ended up.

Although I now had some answers as to why I behaved in the way I did, I was still very much in the early stages of healing. I wish I could say that my odd behaviors vanished overnight or that I'd given up the projected persona I displayed to the world, but I am happy to say I was finally making some headway. One such victory was being able to fully acknowledge my continued masking. I was very aware of what I was doing, but I still didn't know how to remove it.

Ethan was growing up so fast and I was keen to start CBT as quickly as possible. I admit I was still impatient and didn't like to wait for things. Mostly, I didn't want Ethan to grow up with a false and internally miserable father. I did make a conscious effort to get to know him on a deeper level while I waited for CBT. I tried to play more games with him and give him some sense of control over our routine, but in doing so, I often became uptight and overprotective in other areas of our life.

My fear of Ethan being marginalized dominated my thinking during this time. Ethan was a child who simply didn't take the same comfort in adult company as I did when I was his age. When I made this realization, I recognized that my sense of empathy had greatly improved. I even tried to imagine myself as Ethan—he was very small in stature and had his daddy's giant frame casting a shadow over him all the time. I was exactly double Ethan's height and I visualized someone twelve feet eight inches standing over me, and how that might make me feel. It made me feel slightly afraid; would one step out of line trigger the beast? For Ethan, one step into what I perceived to be danger triggered my fears and I had to save him.

With this new self-awareness, the guilt was becoming strong. I hadn't realized how much I had impacted Ethan's life. I still brought my notepad and pen everywhere to take notes of past instances and memories when they came to mind, since I knew from my research that I would have homework and preparation to do for CBT once it started. I was finally at a stage where I was aware of my behaviors, but I didn't have the tools yet to keep them under control. My attitude was slowly starting to shift and I was starting to accept my quirky self and resent my alter ego. It was time for him to go.

CHAPTER 9

I was sitting at work looking over my calendar when I noticed a bold red circle around July 23, Ethan's fourth birthday. By this stage, he was aware that his birthday was on the horizon and was keen to plan it with me. Although I love planning and being organized, I dreaded the thought of Ethan's birthday party. I wasn't looking forward to the noise, the smells, and the chaos, and my fear of not being able to cope with these elements was even worse.

Later at home, I asked him where he wanted to have his party and he triumphantly requested the place we had been for his second birthday. Deep down I had secretly hoped he'd want his party to be at the library or even our home—safe places that I could cope with. I considered dissuading him from his decision but I resolutely decided I had to put Ethan first. In the past, I often avoided situations that didn't fit within my comfort zone, even family events such as these. But those days of avoidance were behind me.

I knew I had to pay a deposit to secure the venue and invited his mum to come with me. Although we had been separated a long time, we always agreed to collaborate for his birthday parties and future milestones. For one reason or another, she couldn't attend so I went on my own.

As I drove across the city, I immediately felt myself having difficulty swallowing and my heart rate started to increase as I neared my destination. Before I knew it I was sitting in the parking lot staring at the building. I remember I could still hear the faint noise of children inside (even from my closed car!) and had sight of the flickering yellow, red, and green lights. It was time to compose myself. Slowly my hand rose to my car door and I made the giant leap of stepping outside the safe confines of my car.

As I slowly approached that front door, the feelings I had experienced at Ethan's last birthday there returned with a rush. With every step the noise got louder and my eyes started to sting like someone had thrown salt water into them. I had devised my plan before heading out: I would enter quickly past the arcade machines and pay the deposit as quickly as I could before fleeing out the door.

I stopped with my hand on that entrance door and looked wistfully back at my car. The thought of running back to the car and making up an excuse started to become very appealing. I couldn't take my eyes off the car and I was about to turn back, but in an uncharacteristic moment of bravado, I breathed deep and walked through that door. Lucky for me, the venue wasn't very busy at that time of day; the only thing that was busy was my brain.

My eyes started stinging profusely because of the bright lights, and the sounds of the arcade games startled me. I rubbed my eyes and kept walking toward the desk to pay the party deposit. My throat had felt closed since leaving the safety of my car and I now found my strangled vocal chords refusing to make words. I somehow provided the reception with my party details and left the deposit on the table. I remember my heart was pounding so hard as I turned to walk away. As I neared the exit, a soft voice called out to me, telling me I'd forgotten my receipt. I found the strength to turn around and take the offered receipt, but once I had it in hand, I bolted through the door and back to the car.

I sat in the car with my head between my hands; I had to have taken at least thirty minutes to allow my senses to stabilize. I didn't know how I would manage the actual birthday party when it came around. From the psychological therapy with Michael, I'd learned that with my sensory overloads, I had the potential to have control or overcome them, due to the fact that I had managed other situations, like a concert, so well. It had always been my view that the sensory overload was a key part of my condition, one that couldn't be treated or "healed," much in the same way a person living with type 1 diabetes will always require insulin. I went home dreading the party; seeing Ethan's joy was no consolation to me.

When I arrived home from work some days later, I opened the door to see a letter addressed to me among the menus and junk mail Ethan hadn't sorted. Even when Ethan went to his mum's, I felt guilty doing his duties, in the same way I would if he did mine. I sat at the table and opened the letter to see that I was being offered my first cognitive behavioral therapy (CBT) session. The appointment would be on the Friday just two days before Ethan's birthday party.

For the remainder of the evening, I researched CBT. I learned that CBT would allow me to discuss the findings from my psychological therapy and learn new ways to cope. Of course I was very skeptical, although I was equally as intrigued.

I informed my mum that my letter of appointment had arrived and she asked me how I felt. I remember telling her that I was very doubtful that it would work. I still felt quite defeated and I told her about my experience when I went to pay the deposit. In my usual and dramatic fashion, I told the story like I had been caught in a hurricane for several months and had to resort to cannibalism. Mum encouraged me to give the therapy a chance and to have an open mind.

I distracted myself by going out and buying all of Ethan's birthday presents, but that only worked for so long. In the early morning hours on the day of the appointment, I lay awake in bed, feeling eager for a change. I had made significant progress in getting to the cause of my issues, particularly how my childhood affected me into adulthood. I couldn't imagine how CBT could suddenly alter my lifetime of quirks, but I was keen to find out.

I arrived on time and waited for the therapist to come and greet me. I realized when I sat in the waiting room that I didn't have a sudden urge to escape. I had come so far and I didn't want to let Ethan or myself down. I was determined to see this through like I did with everything else. I'd struggled through university, a marathon, and Ethan's first few years. I couldn't give up now.

My therapist, who I will call Jane, came to greet me in the waiting room. When she extended her arms, I immediately obliged without giving it a second thought of hugging a complete stranger. She was very cheerful and seemed genuinely pleased to meet me. I was often cautious when people greet me with enthusiasm because I didn't think of myself to be overly interesting.

Jane's clinic room was much different than the room I had met Michael in. It was much more informal and she had a poster of Sigmund Freud on the wall beside her desk. She had all her academic certificates on the wall as well as photographs of her family. Her office was spacious, with the same leather sofas one would find in a Victorian gentleman's club. As I had tastes beyond my years, I fell in love with her office.

After officially introducing herself again, Jane gave me an overview of what the following four weeks would involve. The sessions would take place on a weekly basis and I would have homework in the same fashion as my last therapy. I love a good overview and I hoped to enjoy the sessions as much as I enjoyed the last ones.

Jane asked me if I considered myself to be an awkward man and I answered that I did. She then promptly denied that I was. I jokingly congratulated her on knowing me better than I knew myself and then insisted she was quite wrong. She responded to my adamant denial by hugging me again, which I accepted without hesitation. She told me that I had an ingrained belief that I was awkward but my behavior with her so far suggested otherwise. I was starting to think she could be right. Jane looked at the report that Michael had sent her, which highlighted the low opinion I had of myself. This was something she vowed to change.

She asked me how my mood had been lately and I told her that I was nervous about Ethan's upcoming party. I took a deep breath, and I told her about the experience I'd had two years before. It was the first time I told anyone about what happened that day and the sensory issues I'd had. I told her about my fear that it would happen again at tomorrow's gathering and that I couldn't face seeing Ethan upset at his birthday party.

Jane told me to close my eyes and imagine myself at Ethan's age. She told me to look at myself through Ethan's eyes at his birthday party. In my mind as Ethan, the world seemed magical all of a sudden. I remembered the feeling I had when I played games as a child or played with my toy cars. Through Ethan's eyes, I saw myself standing awkwardly overseeing playtime, complete with my usual blank stare, and shared this observation with Jane. She asked me how I felt when seeing myself stare the way I did. I told her it was quite unnerving.

When I was younger my mother didn't often take me to children's play areas. It frequently led to meltdowns because I couldn't speak. In my imagination as Ethan, I started saying hello to other children around me and this amused me. I couldn't have done this myself when I was younger and I will always remember the void of being unable to vocalize properly. I never thought this way before and it was very emotional for me.

We went deeper into discussion with regard to my relationship with Ethan. I told her that when we are at playgrounds, I tend to stand very close and will speak on his behalf out of fear that he might be an aggressive child like I was. Jane noted that I had felt happy speaking with other children when my imagination allowed me to see the world through Ethan's eyes. She asked me to return to that feeling and imagine being pulled away from the interaction. I told her that this would be quite upsetting.

This was a major breakthrough. For the first time I could see myself as Ethan did. Given my size, it must have been terrifying for other children to approach him with me standing beside him. I was ruining Ethan's playtime due to my own fears and doubts. For once, I wasn't thinking about my own survival, but the feelings of others.

Ethan's party was just two days away, and I recalled the excitement I felt leading up to my own birthday parties as a child. Mum and Dad had always thrown me great parties although they were often at home. My closest family and friends were always present. I loved blowing the candles out on my birthday cake and opening my presents.

For our next exercise, Jane told me go back into Ethan's mind for the party. When I entered the imaginary party as Ethan, she asked me what I could see. I told her I saw other children and that I felt nervous about this. I went on to say that everyone was tall compared to me and that I felt quite uneasy and shy. She asked me if my adult self was nearby, but I couldn't see myself, so I immediately opened my eyes. I couldn't imagine myself not being there and I started to doubt the exercise entirely. Jane told me to persevere and that she would answer my questions at the end.

I returned to Ethan's happy and excited mind, and I tried to make sense of why I wasn't there in his eyes. A fleeting thought came to mind: I could have been cowering in a dark corner because of my hypersensitivity. When I returned to the present room, Jane asked me what my main concern was. I explained how I couldn't find myself at the party and Jane asked if I was sure that was my main concern. I said that it was.

Jane asked me to go back in time and imagine it was my own birthday in the same place. I was back to being four years old; Mum had her giant glasses back and Dad was sporting his moustache again. I told Jane that I was clinging to Mum and I found the venue was much too noisy. I didn't want to stay there and I felt the same sense of dread as I did when I was only small.

We discussed both role-plays and highlighted the obvious difference between the two. I wasn't frightened whenever I was in the venue as Ethan. I didn't recall being frightened because of the noise, or even wanting to flee the scene. For those brief moments walking in my son's shoes, I forgot that I had Asperger's. She advised me that in order to face the birthday party, I would have to try and see the situation through Ethan's eyes. He obviously wanted me to be there and to share his happiness.

I had attached a bad emotional experience to the party venue. Of course, it had always been autism friendly and catered to people of all abilities, but my mind didn't allow me to view it this way. My mind often worked in a way that certain situations and places caused me distress, and it now occurred to me that I could never change the actual situations and places, only how I handled being in them.

Jane went on to explain that a common autistic trait is to see situations literally. My thinking processes were programmed in such a way that my senses heightened and I felt everyone was staring at me. I always had this fear so I often avoided social situations. This session with Jane was one of the first times I felt deep empathy for another human being, and I am so glad it was for Ethan. I couldn't risk him growing up with the belief that I was emotionally absent, and at times overpowering.

My session came to an end and I was quite upset at what I had discovered. In just one session, I had come to realize that my mind (and life) was completely controlled by my desire to feel comfortable and safe. My mind had created barriers, issues, and reasons to always run. Any time Ethan tried to build a deeper relationship with me, I put up barriers around me because I feared that my perceived weaknesses would show. Trying to hide my fears in front of Ethan all the time was exhausting, and probably was what prompted him to ask my mum why I always looked so sad.

My first session had only lasted for an hour, and yet I had made an enormous breakthrough. I couldn't believe what had taken place, and I was completely overcome with sadness. I explained this to Jane, and she told me that what I was feeling was normal given the emotional gravity of the exercise. She reassured me that the realization of empathy is always difficult to come to terms with, but the long-term benefits would be felt by both me and Ethan.

I was given another topic to consider for next week's session: my working life. Jane found it very interesting that I was able to manage my working life quite well. We both chuckled at the fact that of all the careers I could have entered into, I chose one of the most challenging for those with autism. She wanted to better understand my masking behaviors and the character I had created for myself. I was told to write two descriptions: one of myself during working hours and the other outside of working hours. Jane's parting advice to me at the end of the session was to imagine how Ethan would feel if I was visibly incapable of coping during the party.

I went home and thought about the session the entire day. I reflected on the past five years and how my life would have been so simple if I had only learned to see things through the eyes of others. I did some research and I found that a common misconception surrounding Asperger's syndrome is the alleged lack of empathy. I found the choice of phrase quite insulting, almost as if we choose to ignore the feelings of others. It isn't that simple. I have been different my entire life due to my condition; it wasn't my fault nor was it anyone else's. Given the marginalization and stigma I went through, I developed an irrational selfishness that isolated me from everyone.

Without my false persona that I portrayed to the world, I probably would have eventually faded into the background. I was faced with a choice in my childhood: to try and fit in or fade away into obscurity. I imagine many with autism face this decision and it is a terrible one to make. Attempting to fit in could backfire and cause humiliation like it did with me, or fading away can reduce the desire to form healthy relationships with others. I suppose this is reason why we can be considered more like ghosts than people.

The following day, I took Ethan to my mum's house and I shared with her that I had my first therapy session. I didn't go into explicit detail; I didn't want her to think for a moment that I didn't always consider the feelings of others. Of course, she already knew I didn't, but I didn't feel comfortable saying it out loud. Dad took Ethan to the back garden to kick around his new football and I told Mum that I was starting to feel better.

She reminded me kindly that if I had accepted and availed of these treatments many years before, I would have been able to have a happier adulthood. I already knew that I wouldn't regain lost time, but attempting to let go would allow me to cherish the times I had ahead of me. I went into the back garden and kicked the football with Ethan. I wanted to be there with Ethan when he was smiling and having fun, but being there was one thing; joining his happiness was another matter entirely. We had such a nice day and Ethan returned to his mum's house excitedly, knowing his birthday party would be the next day.

I returned home and found myself staring out my bedroom window again. As I contemplated tomorrow's party from behind the safety of my window, I decided that I wanted to go outside. I went for a walk that evening to expend some energy to help me sleep that night. I can't say that I was excited for Ethan's party, but I was determined not to be afraid. As I walked alone that night, I wanted to build up the confidence to go through with Ethan's party and not to let my restless mind take over. I got home, went to bed, and fell asleep very quickly.

I woke up quite early the next day and I experienced the sense of time passing me by quickly: Ethan was now four years old. I thought about the day he was born. It only seemed a matter of weeks ago. I had gone through so much in the last four years that it seemed to last forever in equal measure. I gathered the presents I had bought for him, and I prepared to go to his mum's house to bring them to the party.

When Ethan opened the front door, he was dressed in new clothes for the party and had a giant birthday badge pinned to his shirt. I gave him a big hug and I felt how grown up he was when I hoisted him up in the air. I knew that he would soon be too big to hold and I didn't want his innocence to be ruined by my eternal unhappiness. We got into the car and made our way to the party venue. I would love to say I felt entirely serene and that nothing in the world could harm me, but I did become nervous the closer we got.

My test had come. My nerves started to build and the feeling of my throat closing was starting to happen again. Immediately, I transferred to Ethan's mind, like I did during my therapy session just two days prior. I imagined being so excited that I just wanted to get out of the car and charge headfirst into the party. Knowing Ethan was excited inspired me to get out of the car, unfasten his seatbelt, and take him inside.

I was so afraid of having a meltdown that I squeezed Ethan's hand, but not so hard that he felt pain. It was almost like a silent request for him to stay with me while I faced my fear. We were taking this challenge on together. I made a promise to myself that I wouldn't let go of his hand or let him down. When we arrived inside the sights, smells, and noises were frighteningly familiar. Since my hand was bound in Ethan's, I knew I couldn't place my hands over my ears. I matched his excited and hurried pace toward the party room.

I was immediately overwhelmed inside the children's play area. The noise was starting to trouble me and I sat down right away. I sat and watched Ethan play with his friends and the adults enjoy refreshments. While observing, I tried to visualize Ethan having fun and looking over at me. I didn't imagine him wanting to see my usual sadness. So I tried to put on the bravest face despite the noise hurting my ears.

For the next twenty minutes, I fought the urge to leave and go to the sanctuary of a toilet stall that I had hid in two years ago. I didn't want to risk him looking for me and not being able to find me, so I stayed glued to the chair. When staring up at the soft climbing frame, I called out his name and Ethan ventured nervously toward the safety netting. When he peered down over the railing, I raised my hand to wave and forced myself to smile. When he saw me, he was clearly delighted and waved enthusiastically before running back to play.

I was so proud of this that I naturally couldn't stop smiling. Mum and Dad probably thought I was simply happy that it was Ethan's birthday and I was savoring the occasion, but my happiness had a much deeper meaning. I walked over to the climbing frame and called out for him again. Ethan rushed to see me. I asked him if he was having fun and he answered emphatically that he was. I knew I had got off to a great start and it was halfway through the party. Seeing his smiling face and adoring eyes was so much stronger than the urge to run. When I transferred back to Ethan's mind, I saw that I was being the daddy he longed for.

When it was time for cake, all the children gathered round and started to sing "Happy Birthday" to Ethan. His mum and I approached him with the cake and I noticed the smell of the burning candle. I tried my utmost to smile, and I think I succeeded for the most part. Ethan was delighted that we were both there sharing the moment with him.

Afterward, music boomed and the children played games. The volume of the music was starting to burn my eardrums and I feared relapse. I had come so far that I couldn't fail now. I was edging backward, toward the door, when another parent told me jokingly of their hatred for children's music. I immediately laughed and agreed. Could this parent sense that I was struggling? I can't know for sure, but what I do know is that simple question ensured that I had the courage to stay until the end.

The lights came on to signal that our party was over. I had to restrain myself from jumping in the air with delight, although Ethan was clearly upset. He didn't want his party to end nor to say goodbye to all his party guests. His friends received their slice of cake along with their bag of treats and made their way to the exit. The feeling I had at the end of that party was the feeling I thought I'd achieve when running twenty-six miles—pure elation. Ethan was genuinely proud of both his parents and I could feel it.

Mum and Dad were happy that the party had gone so well and that Ethan had fun. I didn't tell them of my massive victory; not because I didn't want to steal the limelight from Ethan, but rather I was so ashamed of my meltdown two years prior. I wasn't as open back then and I didn't want to sacrifice my pride or feel humiliated. I was euphoric as I held Ethan's hand; we pushed through the blizzard of noise and lights to head back to my car.

It was time to go home and Ethan was clearly tired as he sat in his car seat. On the way home, we stopped for ice cream, but Ethan was so full of food that he couldn't bring himself to eat it. His mum was so happy the party went well and so was I. The staff there had thrown him such a great party that I enjoyed it too! It was a relief to break at least one of the chains that held me down for so long.

It may seem trivial and almost ridiculous to some, but the strength I had to find to survive that party was immense. I never imagined being able to do it, and all it had taken was to try and see the world through Ethan's eyes. I know Ethan may never see, hear, or smell with the same hypersensitivity as I do, but I knew that all he wanted was to feel that I was involved in his special day. That, to me, was enough to find the willpower to retain my composure from when I entered the building until I left.

I left Ethan and his mum back at their house. I grabbed up Ethan for a big hug and he told me he loved his party and couldn't wait to play with all his new toys. He ran into the house but turned to wave at me before he entered the house. I smiled, waved back to him as I got back into my car. I drove home reflecting on the magnitude of the day's breakthrough. The simplest advice from my therapist had helped me overcome the dread and fear that I associated with Ethan's birthday.

When I got home, I had to go straight to bed. The come-down from the euphoria of surviving the party had exhausted me. I lay awake and, for the first time, felt somewhat hopeful. For the duration of the party, I didn't feel like I was different from any of the other parents. I didn't have to transform into someone I wasn't as a coping mechanism. I was delighted. I survived many social situations prior to this party; I'd had good friends, and good working relationships. The difference being, in this situation, I survived using a healthy coping mechanism.

I was looking forward to my next therapy session and what challenge I would overcome next. I felt that if Jane asked me to enroll in an astronaut training program, I would be able to go through with it with ease. For the next couple of days, I was flying high from success. I don't remember ever having felt so elated in my life. I was also feeling slightly guilty about my skepticism prior to attending therapy. I hadn't believed I would be able to program my mind to think in a different way. Boy had I been wrong!

As a child, I never thought I could part company with my toy cars and thought I would never be able to integrate into society in a meaningful way. I now felt at peace knowing that I was experiencing a positive step in securing the relationship I wanted with Ethan. I lay in bed that night hoping he would feel the same, in his own fun way.

Before finally falling asleep, I practiced projecting into Ethan's mind as he lay in his own bed that night. I realized he had just turned four years old and was probably wondering if there was ice cream in my freezer for the next time he was coming over. This made me laugh out loud and it helped me to appreciate that Ethan's psyche was different to mine. I couldn't imagine him analyzing my performance that day—he most likely suspected nothing.

I called Mum to see if she had picked up on my groundbreaking performance at the birthday party. She was delighted that Ethan enjoyed his day and that both his parents enjoyed it too. Mum and Dad have always had a special bond with Ethan and wanted me to have that too. I knew that the birthday party was the start of something special for the both of us. It was almost like falling in love again, but on a much deeper level.

I knew from the moment I received my medication for the first time that I would never be free from Asperger's. It is a lifelong condition that I will still have when I grow old. I had made the mistake of believing that having this condition meant not being able to cope with it. I had held very little hope for myself prior to Ethan's fourth birthday. I often thought I didn't want to live a long life full of hurdles and challenges. Would my life be one challenge after another? The answer to this question was yes, and I now saw that there was hope for me and that I could overcome them in a healthy way. I was learning to face challenges as my true self, and not in other toxic ways to keep my true self hidden.

In the days leading up to my next therapy appointment, I had to focus on the two people that existed in my mind. I was slowly coming to terms with my identity for the first time in my life. The birthday party gave me hope that I could live with my condition in my own way without having to project someone that I wasn't. I envisioned that my next appointment would focus on my false persona. The monster that took refuge within me was starting to run out of time.

CHAPTER 10

I had been on a high after surviving Ethan's birthday party, but that quickly disappeared upon returning to work. My colleagues were surprised and asked as to why I was in such fine mood. I shared pictures from Ethan's birthday party and told them how much fun we had. Until that point, I often showed pictures that portrayed me having fun; in reality I was internally screaming and looking to escape. This time, I showed my pictures on my phone knowing that I was genuinely happy in them. In the past, I had perfected a false smile worthy of any photo shoot.

I was carrying another notepad, and I was very keen to begin the exercise given to me in therapy the week prior. I wrote two headings to demonstrate my working life and home life. I wrote that I didn't mind going to work and largely enjoyed working where I was, even though it was thirty miles away from home. For Ethan's sake, the commute was quite impractical and if there were any childcare arrangements, I couldn't be included given how far I was away from him. If he needed to be picked up from his mum's in an emergency, it was left to my parents to assist while I worked. If I had been able to see through Ethan's eyes two years prior, I probably would not have accepted the job. I enjoyed working with my colleagues and never held any fear of approaching them. I was even able to sit in the staff room and converse freely without fear of judgment, something I was quite puzzled by.

I would often avoid social situations but if I couldn't get out of it, I'd prepare meticulously for any kind of event that didn't involve work. I couldn't understand this at all. How could I fear the company of my own child or my closest friends, and yet not fear my work colleagues? I wrote this point in bold letters in my notepad, so that I'd remember to ask Jane the next time we met. The only fear I identified at work was a sudden change to my preplanned day, although this was the same whenever I was at home.

In the two years I worked there, I had traveled across the country and met many people, none of whom were undergoing the same therapy as I was. Of course, I didn't tell anyone that I was availing of CBT. As my work progressed, I was seeing more clients and I enjoyed supporting them through difficult times. I was so grateful for the support I was receiving outside of work and that my understanding toward others had started to improve.

I was visiting so many vulnerable people throughout a diverse setting. No two cases were the same and I now had a firsthand understanding of the impact mental and psychological illnesses had on other people. In some cases it didn't matter if a client had a lovely home, a supportive family, or lots of money. Their main concern was how their behaviors were impacting those around them, sometimes without their knowledge. Some had been living with traits very similar to mine and had even been given the relatively modern diagnosis of autism, while many others, like myself, had not been given any conclusive verdict during their childhood.

I believed that no two cases were the same but I started to notice that I was being far too literal. Of course I didn't have two clients with the same name or address, but I was finding one similarity: their struggles impacted everyone around them. Both mental illness and autism contain behavioral traits that are difficult to understand. For instance,

I'm unable to simply stop having Asperger's, no matter how many people have told me to stop obsessing and worrying. In a lot of cases, people are unable to stop feeling down or stop hoarding, or whatever their specific issue is. It makes me quite sad to know some families distance themselves from my clients due to a lack of understanding and inability to heal.

I had another striking revelation at work. Every time I visit someone, I take note of their home's exterior from an aesthetic point of view. I have been to houses that were dilapidated and some that were so beautifully Edwardian, they wouldn't look out of place in a period drama film. Naturally, I found the latter homes more aesthetically pleasing. Interestingly, the beautiful, stately homes I visited held the same secrets and sadness as their modest counterparts did. I've visited clients in some of the most beautiful surroundings. Some had many acres of land and lived very successful lives. Seeing a beautiful home exterior and a distraught client inside reminded me of myself sometimes; I had a very different exterior than what was going on inside.

A common theme that I found when supporting my clients was regret. Many admitted to me that they had known of their issues for many years before finally accepting help. Many told me that their refusal to acknowledge their behaviors or accept support hindered them greatly. Had I continued to deny support, I very easily could have found myself in the same situation as the people I support in work. I was able to see what my future might look like if I didn't give my therapy the full attention it deserved.

I immediately thought about my own obsessions and how they caused pain for others. I hadn't allowed my behavior to be changed by anyone, not even my parents. My life had to reach such a low point before I was finally willing to accept help after having refused it for so many years. Now, I was embarking on a journey of my own, starting therapy to make peace with myself and improve my quality of life. Many clients told me their counselors or psychiatrists recommended they speak to a social worker about their circumstances to help them become part of the society they so desperately wanted to stay away from. Many told me that allowing me into their home was part of their therapy and I was delighted to be a part of someone else's victory, having had one of my own just days earlier.

When my appointments finished, I'd thank my clients for allowing me into their home and say that I understood how hard it must have been for them. When I left people's homes, I would pause and look back at the house itself. The house exterior and grounds were often located in a world much different from the one that existed inside—the story of my life.

I was forming relationships much more positively since I started my therapies and I was able to present the real me on social work appointments without openly disclosing my own circumstances. I had often felt professional inadequacy because I couldn't feel the pain of others. In time, I've come to understand that I wasn't a social worker so I could share in my client's pain, but rather I was there to help them overcome it in a positive way.

I summarized my two states of being in my notebook: I was confident and outgoing at work while I was withdrawn at home. Some links still existed—planning my days, struggling with the unknown, and the perceived barrier that existed between Ethan and me. My mind often raced and it could cause distraction from tasks at home; this existed in both scenarios, too.

I arrived to see Jane for my second appointment and I was very keen to tell her my findings. I explained the behaviors I'd observed in myself at work and outside of work, and she told me that I was a typical case of masking. Jane explained rather well what masking was using the work of Vincent Van Gogh. She explained that many of his paintings depict cheerful subjects such as scenery or flowers. Van Gogh was painting a world that he could happily exist in, despite his obvious mental illness. Jane explained that in some respects, I was doing the same thing—I wanted others to see my world in a different light and color. It was explained to me that this behavior can often be dangerous and self-destructive. Spending so much time trying to project a positive image restricts time better spent improving oneself. A light bulb switched on for me and I couldn't have agreed more. I was spending so much time painting a certain image of myself out to the world and the ultimate losers were Ethan and me.

I was glad to finally be spending time working on my internal emotions instead of trying aimlessly to prove myself as someone different. Many clients I had visited earlier in the week had done exactly the same, the difference being most waited for so long and faced many more consequences.

Jane told me to close my eyes and imagine being back at school at five years old. I was sitting in my tiny red chair, unable to speak, with my classroom assistant sitting beside me. Jane asked me how I was feeling and I considered the immediate frustration I felt having an adult sit with me in the classroom. Nobody else in my classroom had an assistant and it caused me immense irritation. I knew I needed the help, even as a child, as my verbal skills were simply not good enough yet. Jane asked me to try and explain my condition to my classmates. I pictured myself walking to the front of the room and trying to speak, but I couldn't. My mind allowed me to hear a snigger and I became quite angry. I was unable to tell the class even in this mind exercise, and I believed I'd failed the task.

I told Jane that I simply couldn't do it; my communication skills were much too limited at this age. I was able to speak in the last exercise whenever I envisioned I was Ethan, but when I was myself, I couldn't. I projected the scenario very literally, like I do with almost anything. By the age of five, I had a better vocabulary range, although not large enough to fit in with my peers. I resented my classmates in my imaginary scenario because they would never be able to understand me. Jane suggested that I was likely feeling like this at the time and I agreed. I imagined other children being well-behaved, respecting other people's ways, and I was quite envious of them. She asked me to go back into my mind, but this time I was to go to the playground. I was standing next to my teacher while I was watching everyone else playing. Jane suggested I approach another child to join in a game. I tried to imagine the situation but I simply couldn't, which was beyond frustrating. I was reassured that I hadn't failed the task and that we'd revisit this in a later session.

It was time for another exercise and Jane asked me to close my eyes and begin my journey from my house to my office. Of course, this wasn't in real time and I focused on how I would normally feel on the thirty miles of road leading to my office door. I explained that I felt no anxiety and that I was mentally planning how my day would go. I often spoke aloud in the car to allow my thoughts to process. I greeted everyone with my usual smile and sat at my desk. Jane brought me back to the room and asked me how I was feeling. I confirmed that I was feeling fine and that I would typically be ready for the working day as I sat down at my desk.

I thought about the personalities of my colleagues. I had only good thoughts about them—we all worked well together and I enjoyed being in their company. It was then that Jane asked me to do the impossible. She told me to imagine that I was in the staff room, and I had to announce to everyone that I had Asperger's. I immediately refused and told her that I could never do such a thing. Jane reminded me that I was in a safe place to do so and the only people in the room were me and her. My secret was still safe. I breathed deeply with my eyes closed and found the courage to request the attention of everyone in the staff room. I told them that I had something to share and I remember everyone staring at me. I must have been unconsciously making facial expressions of discomfort as I heard Jane's voice encouraging me to continue. I announced to the room that I had Asperger's and that part of my therapy was being open about my condition. Without my mind allowing it, my team was suddenly applauding and they all approached to hug me. I wasn't ready for this kind of response—in real life or in my mind's eye.

Without being prompted, I opened my eyes and told Jane exactly what had happened. She was so proud of me. She gave me her sincere congratulations and told me to speak about how I was feeling. I was in such disbelief that my mind had allowed the response that it did and I was now struggling to translate my emotions into words for Jane. I hadn't felt like I was being judged and I had felt like an enormous burden had been lifted from me. As I sat on the couch in Jane's office, I suddenly felt the adrenaline rush through my body and I smiled. I asked her what the purpose of this activity was, and she told me that the pain of childhood memories created a negative thought process in my brain. I already knew that my childhood had deeply affected me into adulthood, but not the extent that it actually did.

In my working life, I was able to integrate into working environments much easier as I was able to communicate. As a child, I couldn't speak and nobody could understand the condition I had, so I imagine that had been difficult for them too. Given that I was now working on a mental health team complete with psychiatric nurses, it dawned on me that they probably knew I was on the autism spectrum. They all witnessed how my desk was arranged in my own particular way and I required the clerical staff to complete my correspondences and paperwork in a way that I liked and specified. I remembered a colleague telling me many months before that my files were slightly different to the rest of the team. I remember replying that I simply liked them being done in a certain way and the discussion was in no way confrontational. The truth is, I didn't feel judged at work; in fact I always felt at home there.

Jane agreed with this assessment. In my mind, I had created a safe space, and so I allowed my colleagues into it. I immediately felt sad that I hadn't managed to build a safe space for Ethan to enjoy with me. When I mentioned this point, Jane returned to the first exercise and explained that communicating with children was an obvious mental block that I had put in place. I hadn't outgrown the fear and anxiety from my childhood and it existed in my mind when I was standing in the imaginary playground. When approaching Ethan, I was afraid of rejection and this caused me to stop trying. In two therapy sessions I had two breakthroughs and I knew I was making real progress.

As time was running out with our session, I was asked to complete a very daunting task for the following week. Jane asked me if I would feel comfortable speaking to a colleague about having Asperger's— I immediately froze. The exercise in her office was one thing, but this was an entirely different matter. I immediately raised my concern and she reminded me that my mind had generated a positive response when I told the whole team during the exercise. Although I generally have trust issues due to my fear of humiliation, I agreed to tell one person and one person only. I couldn't believe what I had just signed up to do and immediately wanted to reject this proposal, but instead I just smiled and left.

Ethan came to stay with me that night and we sat at the table drawing pictures together. I asked him to draw a picture of our new house and he got right to work. Once finished, he proudly shared it with me—he had drawn himself and the house but nothing else. I asked if he wanted to draw me with him but he declined. He decided that his masterpiece did not need any more alterations. I thought I had become his best friend following his birthday party, and I started to fear that wasn't the case. Ethan went to bed after hearing his bedtime story, so I retreated to my room to reflect on my task for the following week.

I couldn't possibly tell someone I had Asperger's; why would I do such a thing?! I imagined the reality of telling someone and I immediately felt the rejection coursing through my veins. I allowed my last victory at Ethan's birthday party to become overshadowed by my own self-doubt. I had completed two out of my four sessions and made significant progress; I couldn't allow myself to continue my destructive ways. I reflected on my visits to clients with the beautiful homes and I imagined the scenario if I were in their shoes. I am sure if they realized they needed help and disclosed this to someone, their lives would have been entirely different. Without being in Jane's office, I mentally pictured myself at some of my work visits and putting myself in the place of my clients. I am sure in cases where my clients realized they had a behavior or trait that caused family or parental relationships to break down, they would have happily reversed time to undo the damage. Many would have accepted more help and support if they were given the chance to repeat their lives. This inspired me to continue with my own therapy with determination.

I knew I had to complete the task that Jane had assigned and by Monday morning I had planned out what I was going to say. I even prepared some responses given their possible reaction. One colleague was particularly close to me and I decided she was the one I would tell. I had only ever told my university tutor that I had Asperger's and nobody else since. I was feeling nervous but also determined. I was making so much progress that I had to see this challenge through to the end, whatever that may be. I arrived at work and composed myself for the conversation I would have with my selected colleague.

As we sat in our office, I started organizing my desk in its usual fashion: notebook in the bottom right corner, phone placed near my left hand, and pens in the penholder with all their lids pointing upward. I looked over at my "victim's" desk, which sat adjacent to mine, and remarked at how messy it was. She told me that she keeps her files on the desk in order to prevent going in and out of her filing cabinet and was jealous at how I was always able to keep my desk in such good order. With a deep breath, I naturally added that the reason why my desk was so organized was because I had Asperger's.

I can't always read facial expressions, although she didn't seem immediately surprised. She told me she had noticed some of my traits throughout our time working together and wondered if there was an underlying reason. I confirmed that there was.

My heart pounded as I spoke openly for the first time. I was being the person I had always wanted to be, myself. I explained to her that having my desk organized a certain way gave me comfort, which in turn allowed me to get through the working day. I also added that any interruptions could cause me to become annoyed. She acknowledged that she'd seen this behavior before when a crisis call would come to me and she reiterated that the atmosphere in the room would alter when a sudden change was made to my day. There it was—she had always known, yet was always kind to me.

I didn't feel in any way judged and the sensation of the burden lifting from my body was the same as when I was in Jane's office doing the exercises. I immediately became somewhat defensive and demanded to know if any other colleagues had noticed the same traits as she had. She gently told me that some other colleagues had made passing comments throughout my time working there. I was slightly embarrassed to learn this, though really, it shouldn't have been much of a surprise. I opened up to her about not wanting to tell anyone out of fear that nobody would understand. Her kind demeanor turned into laughter and I became confused. I immediately thought she was laughing at me. Through her laughter, she told me how it was impossible to hide having Asperger's in a building full of psychiatric nurses, mental health social workers, and a consultant psychiatrist. I have to admit that I also found this quite funny, although my pride was dented somewhat.

I had accomplished an enormous step; I finally had told someone the truth about myself. I couldn't believe I had actually gone through with it, and was quite relieved at how good it had gone. This was quite an achievement for me and was an important step in making the changes in order to build a better relationship with Ethan. After that day, my coworker and I never spoke of it again nor did I tell anyone else that I worked with. I had more important people to tell.

When my third therapy session arrived later in the week, Jane eagerly asked me if I had gone through with the task and I confirmed that I had. She applauded me and told me that she knew I could do it. I expressed my disbelief at what I had done and how the invisible weight on my shoulders had reduced. Jane commented that she noticed that my entire body language had changed; it wasn't as closed and aggressive as it was when we began our sessions. As I had removed a barrier, I was speaking much more openly without the heavy burden.

We further discussed how this breakthrough would benefit my relationship with Ethan, given this was my primary concern when I started this journey. I didn't know how telling my work colleague the truth would impact Ethan, but Jane explained that I seemed much more approachable and happy, and that Ethan would sense this. I remained slightly skeptical but I agreed to continue on with the session. I mentioned our playtimes and that I always felt unsure as to what to do during these times. I now knew that I often placed barriers between Ethan and me, all because I had been hopeless at communicating with other children when I was at school. This learned habit of putting up a wall to protect myself had followed me into parenthood. I feared rejection far too much. I told Jane that when we went to the park I would constantly hover near him and eliminate any threats that I perceived to be real. I remembered the time when I took him to the park and I stopped him playing with another child because of my own fear of Ethan facing the same rejection as I did.

We discussed Ethan further and I admitted to Jane that I knew I had been terribly unwell for the majority of his life. I explained that I'd stopped taking my medication and had completely regressed to using my dangerous, ill-placed coping mechanisms that I'd created. I told her that as a parent, I believed I had to lead his playtime to ensure his safety. While this is technically true, I was taking this to another level that caused more harm than good. I wasn't allowing Ethan to grow and progress naturally as a child should.

We discussed my relationships with both of my parents and I had only positive things to say. My mum fought heroically to keep me at the school I was in, and my dad took me to Derry City FC games. I had so many happy memories as a child; my parents allowed me to grow as a person, something I was just now recognizing I wasn't doing for Ethan.

Jane advised me to think of our daily routine. I told her our entire routine, how things went when we were together and how the routine gave me comfort. She suggested that I mix it up and allow Ethan to come up with our routine as an experiment, but I soundly rejected this idea because I was the parent and had to establish boundaries. She reminded me that behavioral boundaries could still be in place, but I had to allow Ethan to step out of my shadow and into the light.

It was very difficult to accept any changes in my routine and I was initially very hesitant, but I agreed to try. Our therapy session was over and I had to come back next week to discuss my findings for our next session together. By this stage, I had complete trust in Jane as she'd always kept me on the right path.

Ethan returned that night, and I immediately asked him what he'd want to do the following morning when we got up. I was used to planning all our activities as one of my parental duties, but I reluctantly handed it over to Ethan for the first time. He told me he wanted to go to the park after breakfast and bring his toy cars. I agreed with this initially, although I secretly hoped he would forget by morning so I could resume my planning duties. Little did I realize that this was a first step in learning to let go completely. I was developing trust of other people and was willing to take risks to achieve results. Before I started therapy I had thought that if I wasn't in control or things were done differently to how I liked them, bad things would happen.

I was awakened the following morning by an excited, shadowy figure standing at the foot of my bed. Ethan immediately reminded me that we had agreed to go to the park after breakfast. I sighed, resigned. We would actually be doing something that I hadn't planned and I had to fight to stop myself from coming up with an excuse to not do what he wanted. It is so difficult to explain this emotion—I know some would view this as controlling but I can't emphasize enough the feeling of dread and sadness that overcomes me when events don't run how I imagined them to.

We put on our coats and we set off toward the park, only a short drive from our house. We entered the play park and I went to sit on a bench to watch. Ethan followed and asked what I was doing. I told him that he should go play in the park but could come over to me if he had any problems. He excitedly ran off and I kept my eye on him the entire time. He ran around the park with his arms outstretched like the wings of a jumbo jet. He had the space and freedom to move and was exercising it with much enthusiasm. He'd often look over at me to check in, and I'd wave to him with a smile. Internally, I was forcing myself to remain on that bench and not to go with my instinct to follow him wherever he went. I kept remembering my last therapy session; I had to let Ethan grow and let go of my fear.

Ethan eventually sat down on the ground and brought out his toy cars. Another child noticed and approached him. I watched with bated breath as to what Ethan would do. I now recognized how I had always reacted aggressively whenever approached as a child and didn't want this child to get hurt, as I assumed Ethan may have the same reaction as I'd always had. The child sat beside Ethan and they greeted one another. They started playing with their own cars and were speaking the language of playtime: a language I never understood. I felt myself standing and starting to walk toward them but a sudden wind came up and stopped me in my tracks. I sat back down again, tilted my head back, closed my eyes, and breathed deeply. I knew I would have to get used to Ethan doing this sort of thing if he was ever going to grow up. I sat like this for a while and when I finally opened my eyes Ethan was standing in front of me—he was ready to go home and asked if I would carry him on my shoulders back to the car. I agreed and we laughed together all the way back to the car.

When we got home, Ethan asked if he could pick the activity again for the next morning. He was pushing his luck and I wanted to decline, but when I saw the sparkle in his eyes, I was curious to find out what it was he wanted to do. He told me he wanted to swim. He always loved the swimming pool and I hadn't taken him for quite some time. I agreed and he went to bed with a smile.

Upon waking, Ethan ran into my room and asked me if I had our swimming gear ready. I emphatically said that I had it beside the front door, ready to go. So we went swimming and I was happy to have an excuse to stay with him the entire time. I wasn't foolish enough to allow him to enter the swimming pool alone. He clung to my back as I swam through the water and he giggled with excitement. When Ethan went home that evening, he gave me a hug and ran into his mum's house. I loved seeing Ethan happy. I realized that nothing bad had happened when I allowed him to choose the activities we did together. I couldn't wait to see him smile again; it was becoming my new addiction.

Ethan's mum texted me and asked me if I could keep him for an additional night that week as she would be out of town. I hesitated, as this was outside of my routine, but I remembered how happy Ethan had been in deciding our activities, so I agreed. When Ethan was dropped off at my house, it was pouring rain so we couldn't go outside that evening. I asked Ethan what he wanted to do and he told me he wanted to draw pictures with me at our table again. When Ethan showed me his new masterpiece I was completely overcome—he had drawn me with a smiley face.

CHAPTER 11

For the first time since Ethan was born, we were bonding in the way that I had always wanted. I always longed for closeness with him, which wasn't there before, but now I had it. I was starting to see things differently since starting my therapy—before I was so worried about my condition and how nobody could find out. I had gone from being quite secretive and ritualistic to being much more transparent in the space of just a few weeks. I had the most amazing weekend with Ethan, enjoying every second of it.

My last therapy session was on the horizon and I was told that this would be a longer session than usual. My sessions were an hour long, but the final one would be an hour and a half. I wrote in my notepad throughout the week about how I enjoyed seeing Ethan happy and that he was now involved in deciding our routine. It likely seems absurd to imagine a child not being involved in planning their activities, but I was born with a condition that did not allow me to see things as clearly as everyone else. My rituals, quirks, and behaviors had always been non-negotiable up to this point, and I didn't allow Ethan, or anyone else for that matter, to negotiate with me. I was unable to read situations and, to a degree, I still struggle with this. I had learned to try and that's all that matters.

Watching Ethan play in the park was a nice feeling, although I can often have mixed emotions that I can't interpret. I'd watch him innocently play with another child and I couldn't put into words what my sentiment was. As I was writing in my notepad, a thought occurred to me: I was feeling quite envious. Ethan was able to integrate and play with other children, something I could not do at his age. It was nice to know he was able to do what I couldn't, although the feeling of envy overshadowed my pride in him

My final therapy session arrived on Friday morning and I was quite nervous. I was making significant progress between therapies, but I knew I would be on my own afterward. I wasn't sure that four weeks would be enough to eliminate twenty-seven years of Jude Morrow. I understood that I'd never be free of Asperger's (no one could be—it's fundamentally a part of a person's makeup). As much as I wanted to be the same as everyone else, I knew that I never would be.

When I arrived and sat on Jane's leather sofa, she brought me a cup of coffee and asked me how my week had been. I explained that I'd followed her advice in allowing Ethan to take some control over our activities and that we'd both had a positive experience. I told her that the highlight of the week had been when Ethan drew me with a smiling face, something he hadn't done before. I talked about how what we were working on at that moment had actually started after Ethan asked my mum why I always looked so sad, and that it led to kick-starting my healing journey.

When asked how I felt about myself, I answered honestly that I still felt a large void within me. It was a feeling I couldn't put into words though. I told Jane that I had felt the void whenever I saw Ethan playing in the park, and that it made me feel quite guilty. She explained that the feeling was normal given the childhood I'd had. My suspicions were confirmed that my childhood anxieties still very much existed. The feeling of isolation was strong and in order to move beyond this and have a positive future, I would have to let go of my past.

We continued by discussing the positive relationship I had with my parents and all the struggles they faced with me when I was growing up. I recalled a conversation I'd had with my mum several weeks earlier: She told the story of a time she took me to see a specialist pediatrician. I wasn't sleeping at night (apparently I hadn't slept well for years), and she had become exhausted. She fought for an appointment and was eventually offered one due to her perseverance. We arrived at the hospital and I was terribly agitated. I wouldn't sit down and I ran around the waiting room screaming and shouting. Nurses from other clinics looked at me with annoyance and one even told my mum to try and keep me quiet.

I guess nothing worked, though, and I continued to run rampant around the waiting room until the pediatrician finally came out to collect us. Once we arrived in the room, I promptly started to destroy his office. I threw all of his paperwork on the floor and even stuffed paper towels down his sink. Mum explained to the doctor how she was constantly struggling to cope with my behavior and that I was causing her so much emotional pain. I couldn't verbalize properly at this time, so I vented my frustration often with destructive actions that impacted everyone around me. When Mum told me about this experience, I couldn't actually recall the incident, although I had been very young. Mum had told me this story previously, but I hadn't thought about it the same way as I did now, now that I was in therapy.

Jane, with her boundless wisdom, immediately found the link. She believed I had an unspecified emotion that I still couldn't verbalize. She further elaborated that a trigger for aggression in children with autism is the feeling of being misunderstood. My IQ had never been in doubt, even though I couldn't speak and so was unable to explain how I was feeling. If at that time I'd had the cards with facial expressions on them, I may have been able to communicate more clearly and positively.

Emotional processing for those with autism works much differently. It is the single biggest challenge we face and I can't describe the feeling of not being able to make sense of what I am thinking. Due to this, I often question if my feelings are wrong for the situation I am in and it's exhausting. The general public also finds it quite difficult to understand how a person with autism emotionally processes things and I would often be asked about how it's possible that I can't differentiate between happiness and sadness. It is something that those described as being "neurotypical" can never fully understand, much in the same way those who see the full color spectrum can't understand what it's like to be color-blind and to never see certain colors correctly.

I sat with Jane reflecting on all of this, and my gut skeptical response started to emerge. After today, my therapy would be over, but I still had so many years of frustration to process. Autism is much more publicized now and awareness levels are high among the general public, although there is still a sea of ignorance to navigate through in order to survive. Jane told me that all she could do was to show me how to live (and flourish) with autism.

Jane asked me if I was ready for our first exercise and I confirmed that I was. She told me she'd gained a brief overview of my struggles from Michael's report, but she wanted to hear more from me. I described a childhood where I was often alone since I wasn't keen on mixing with other children. At times I felt my only friend was my sister Emily. I felt so different and I didn't feel I was good enough to mix with them. Jane asked if this was through my own choice or if I had been told explicitly that I couldn't play with other children. I confirmed that it had been my own choice because I didn't know how to fit in.

She asked me if I could recall a child specifically telling me that I couldn't play with them. I wasn't able to remember any specific incidents, although I could recall the feeling of coldness that would sweep over and repel me from approaching other children. She asked if any of these children that I had kept back from had smiling faces, and would I have found it easier to approach them if they did smile. I couldn't find a definitive answer to Jane's questions since I struggled to answer questions about something that happened twenty-two years ago. I wasn't sure if I had any specific issues that stopped me playing, other than the cold, uncomfortable feeling.

When asked about how I felt about having a classroom assistant with me throughout school, I became upset. I was still in the mind frame of blaming the educational system for singling me out and making me different. I still couldn't quite understand why my educators believed I was a risk to my classmates and myself due to my obsessive tendencies at the time. I clearly still held resentment despite the growth and understanding I was gaining of my situation. I described to Jane how I hadn't liked having a classroom assistant with me at all times while it wasn't necessary for the other children. My academic work has never been an issue, only my behavior, and I still felt annoyed that I needed "help" despite being equal in some respects.

That said, I have always spoken highly of my classroom assistant from my earliest school days. She would often praise me and speak to me when nobody else would. I enjoyed her company and she was always kind to me. Even in my teenage years I felt more comfortable conversing with adults than I did with my peers. It was very difficult to explain to Jane, but I would compare it to having a comfort blanket. I have always sought out these adult connections due to feeling reassured by their maturity.

I told Jane how I was confused as to how I could feel so positively about the classroom assistant despite also having bad sentiments because of what having her company meant to my younger self. I had such conflicting emotions, hating feeling different from everyone else in my class. The assistant certainly saw my potential though, even before many of my teachers did.

Upon hearing this, Jane explained to me that the teacher assistant's role would have involved befriending me and making me feel included. We then discussed my other teachers and the one that stood out for me was my primary 5 teacher. He was so kind to me and allowed me to participate in extracurricular activities like the school plays. It was evident from my telling Jane of this time that I enjoyed having responsibilities and feeling included.

After discussing my schooling for quite some time, one thing became apparent: I had many emotional scars from my early school days. I hadn't spoken about them before, but when I did with Jane, it became abundantly clear that I resented the child I had been. I viewed myself as the odd, aggressive, and emotional child that was prone to tears. Until starting my sessions, reflecting back on my childhood was never an option for me—it was a door in my life that I had firmly closed. The shame and resentment I felt toward myself as a child greatly affected me as an adult.

It was very difficult discussing these issues out loud, and I often asked Jane if we could move on, but she wouldn't let me. She told me that this was an issue I had to face, and it was the one that would be most challenging. I had overcome my fears surrounding Ethan, and the final challenge was to overcome myself.

We then moved on to my teenage years. They weren't as troublesome for my parents as my early schooling, but my social difficulties still very much existed. I recognized I still did this, the act of going out of my way to impress others, and that this stemmed from having felt so inadequate for years in my youth. I had made it my life's work to fit in with my peers, yet my efforts often backfired. By the age of twelve, I was in secondary school and I felt I had to make an impression. I still needed support, and the school had great resources available, but this was difficult for me to accept in the testosterone-filled environment of an all-boys school.

Jane understood my reasons for refusal, given my constant desire to fit in with the other boys. I imagine my secondary school days would have been much more pleasant if I had accepted the support I needed. But by then, I was of the age to provide or withdraw consent and I would often refuse any help that was offered to me.

I tried to assign blame for this, but Jane did not accept this for one minute. She told me, rather bluntly, that I had to take some responsibility for my past actions. This was very hard to hear but I knew, deep down, that she was right. My mum always said the same thing to me, even now as an adult.

When discussing my early life in more detail with Jane, it became very obvious that I viewed my life negatively. I had so many chances to speak about the few friends I'd made over the years, or the happy times with my youth group, even gaining my graduate degree. But my focus was completely narrowed by my early hardship so that I couldn't enjoy my life in the present.

Talking it over with Jane, it became clear that I had so many opportunities to integrate and make happy memories, but my fear won out and so I'd often walk away. It all boiled down to the fact that I basically still feared that the awkward child I had been would expose me. Jane identified my inner child as the source of my pain and we had to make that right. It was time to close my eyes again and take on our final exercises.

I was asked to transport myself back in time once again, to our apartment overlooking the city. My cars still sat proudly on the windowsill and I could see Mum sitting in the living room. I told Jane that I couldn't remember the exact layout of the house or colors and this disturbed me, but I was told the exact details of the house didn't matter.

Jane explained that I wouldn't be carrying out the exercise in the eyes of my younger self, but from my eyes as an adult. So I reimagined standing in the room, looking at myself lining up my cars on the window. I saw a glass of milk sitting beside me, and I could see the view out the window. I was so tempted to interact with my younger self but I was strictly told not to do this.

I was asked to allow myself as a child to go to the kitchen table for one of my speaking lessons. Mum then joined me and she was sitting opposite me—I was so small compared to her and I held a blank expression. I was able to understand her command to go to the kitchen table and sit down. Mum was holding cards and mouthing a word to me. Mum said it aloud and was trying to get me to repeat it. Mum pleaded with me to speak; she knew I could do it if I tried.

Without warning, I saw myself sweeping all of Mum's prompt cards off the table and pushing my chair to the floor in anger. My adult self wanted to intervene but I had to stick to Jane's instructions, so I stood on the threshold of the kitchen and observed. My younger self screamed and ran back to the safety of his toy cars while Mum sat and sobbed.

This was how I imagined things to be and I opened my eyes to return to the present. Jane asked if I actually remembered an incident exactly like this, but I couldn't say for certain. I imagine my mum could write her own book on my first three years of life; I don't believe it would make for pleasant reading. I always knew my behaviors had upset Mum to the point of tears, but she had never given up on me.

Through this exercise, I had only witnessed one such incident, but clearly there had been many over the years. I couldn't believe my mum had survived me doing this multiple times per day. I also apparently only slept for three hours per night. I had always respected Mum and Dad for what they had done and still did to support me, but this exercise brought it to a much deeper level.

Jane asked me to return to the situation and to talk while I was "walking" around the house. As an adult in an imaginary scenario, I found I was afraid to approach myself as a child. I didn't know how he, or my mind, would react given the meltdown I'd only just witnessed minutes before. I went into the kitchen and saw Mum's glasses sitting on the kitchen table, and the destruction the younger Jude had left behind. Without being prompted, I imagined kneeling down and starting to pick up all the things that little me had thrown on the ground, and placing them neatly back on the table.

Jane asked me to sit opposite Mum. I pulled over a small chair and sat opposite her. I remember I couldn't face seeing her upset while I sat there. I still didn't know what to do; I didn't know if I should reach for her hand or try to give her a hug. I just uttered that I was sorry, and that I felt guilty because she was upset. Mum, in her forgiving and gentle way, said it was okay and then left the kitchen.

Mum walked over to little Jude, who was much more interested in the cars. Mum sat beside me and started to play. I watched as the two of them sat in silence by the windowsill playing with cars. It was quite uplifting to see Mum coming to play with me, without a shred of anger. With the sound of Jane's voice it was time to come back to the room.

I described my feeling of helplessness at not being able to console my crying mum. I wished I could have done more. We discussed emotions in greater depth, both from my perspective and the perspective of others. Jane reminded me that with any type of autism, understanding internal emotions is very difficult. I still have issues with this and I probably always will. Jane reached for my hand and told me that this wasn't my fault.

When someone I love becomes emotional in my company, I can often become confused as to what I should do. Being able to comfort someone who is upset comes naturally to most—to me it doesn't. Instead, I would often do incorrect things to try and compensate for this and I can't describe the difficulty this brings. No matter how much one researches Asperger's syndrome, nobody will ever understand how difficult this is unless one lives through it.

No matter how much pain someone feels in my presence, I feel terrible that I can't offer much in the way of comfort other than a listening ear. The same goes for anger or frustration—I find it so difficult to read body language and this limitation obviously existed when I was young. I couldn't know how my mum was feeling at any given time and it has always upset and frustrated me.

I looked out the window of Jane's office, trying to hide that I was becoming upset, but I failed. I told Jane about when I was training for my marathon and the numerous injuries I received. Ethan always knew when I was in pain and was able to see through any brave face I'd put on. I'd be hobbling along sandy beaches and parks, trying to keep up with my excited and inquisitive son. Even then, he knew to slow down when he saw I was struggling. I felt ashamed I couldn't have done this for my own mum when I was small.

I already knew my insecurities from childhood were stunting my progress into adulthood. I even knew this deep down before I started therapy, although the extent to which these childhood anxieties were now impacting my life only became clear that day with Jane. She then asked me a very interesting question: she asked me if I had forgiven myself for the way I was. I couldn't answer immediately, but then I told her that I hadn't.

With a deep breath it was time to close my eyes again for my final exercise. Jane explained that in this exercise I'd be working toward removing my final barrier to happiness and forgiving my inner child. I was instructed by Jane to clear my mind. She then told me to stand outside my primary school gates as an adult. With my eyes closed and an emotional breath, it was time to heal.

I remember standing outside the school gates looking at the exterior of the school. I put my hands to my face to feel my beard to ensure I was an adult. I looked down at my tan leather shoes and because of my adult height, I was able to peer over the railings to look into the flower-beds at the front of the school. I glanced around and didn't see anyone else. I described the sensation as isolating and scary to Jane.

I mentioned to Jane the fact that I couldn't hear any noise whatso-ever. No cars were passing by and I stood all alone as I stared at my old primary school. I sighed and started walking toward the entrance gate of the school. I approached the playground; playtime sounds suddenly hit me and I could vividly see everyone playing. I was able to see the colors of the hopscotch game painted on the ground and the sound of the football bouncing off the playground wall.

I navigated through the sea of playing children and I started to feel very nervous. The sound of the football constantly hitting the wall and the schoolgirls' constant screaming as they played was starting to irri-tate me. I was lucid enough to know I could control the imaginary situation so I turned the volume off. Jane agreed that I could do this and asked me to proceed.

I recognized my teacher and the small black-haired boy standing beside her—it was me. I was looking around the playground frantically, and at times the teacher would put her arm around me. I didn't see any-one approaching me or vice versa. In my adult body, disbelief flooded me as I watched younger Jude. I couldn't do now what I couldn't do then. I still couldn't make sense of the hectic situation. As children raced around the playground, I stood there—young and older Jude—invisible to them.

The bell sounded and all the students assembled in their class lines, waiting for the teachers to bring everyone inside. I watched the children get into formation and lost sight of myself amongst the crowd. When all the classes were walking past me toward the doorway into the school, I waited for my class. My teacher led the class and my younger self back into the school. I was at the front of the line holding my teacher's hand while my classmates marched in single file behind us. I remembered almost every classmate and how they looked back then.

I now stood on the playground alone. I asked Jane where I should go next. She told me to go back into the school and go wherever I wanted to. I walked into the school and couldn't believe how much of it I remembered. Upon entering, there was a long corridor leading to the stairs to the second floor. I walked along the corridor and could even imagine hearing the echo of my hard leather shoes as I went.

I climbed the stairs and went toward the room where I went for individual work with my classroom assistant. I reached the door and stared at the translucent glass on the door before slowly opening the door to go inside. As I entered the room, it appeared much smaller than I remembered it being. As a small child it had seemed so vast.

I saw myself sitting at a table drawing a picture. I couldn't make out what the picture was, but I noticed my classroom assistant sitting beside me. She was speaking and I didn't say much back to her. I was stating the names of colors and shapes, but nothing in the way of flowing conversation. The atmosphere in the room felt so positive and I experienced a warm feeling as I watched myself sitting in that chair, drawing innocently.

My classroom assistant was giving me praise and my facial expression toward her was one of warmth. I remembered we'd always had an understanding; she had patience with me that a teacher in a class with thirty other children couldn't have had. I was only one pupil, but still an extremely complex one. It occurred to me then that Ethan was four, and it was very surreal seeing myself so close to his age.

Physically, I was much taller as a child than Ethan, and I had jet-black hair compared to Ethan's light brown. I noticed how awkwardly

I was sitting and when I suddenly put my head down on the desk, my classroom assistant didn't ask me to sit up. I'm not sure if this actually ever happened in real life back then, although my mind allowed the situation to play out. It was clearly a safe place that was structured by me and not by the classroom assistant. My struggles restricted my ability to follow the teacher's plan for that day, so I needed time to learn in my own way.

My classroom assistant told me it was time to go back to my classroom and smiled as she held the door open for me to go through. The pair closed the door behind them and I remained in the room as an adult. I described the room to Jane and how the crayons had been left on the table. My picture was still on the table and I walked over to look at it. I had drawn myself, Mum, Dad, and Emily outside our house with a large sunshine in the top right-hand corner.

Jane then asked me to visit my classroom for a final time. I knew what this meant, so I tidied the imaginary crayons into the imaginary box and placed them in a drawer. My Asperger's is such that even imaginary spaces for a therapy exercise needed to be organized to my liking. I looked around the room for final time and then closed the door behind me to go downstairs to my classroom.

I actually decided to run down the stairs. I remembered running down the stairs when I attended the school and being told to stop. I always ran up and down stairs—at times I'd trip and fall, but I never learned to slow down. I reached the first floor and walked toward my classroom. I walked past the hall where the school plays were taking place and I saw myself on the stage, narrating our school play. I cringed at my childlike voice and didn't wish to stay and watch for too long. I couldn't see Mum and Dad among the crowd but I knew they were in there.

I continued down to my first-year classroom, passing the numerous other classrooms I would eventually sit in during my other years at the school. I looked at all the books on the shelves and the artwork on the walls. I noted to Jane that these classrooms were empty, when in reality they should have been bursting with life. No teacher, no pupils, just silence.

I approached my classroom and I saw the row of coat pegs outside the door. The neat row of coats, that my younger self probably organized, seemed so small. I saw the coat peg with my name on it and a picture of a car. I told Jane that my teacher couldn't have chosen a better image for me to place my coat beside.

I opened the door and tried to take in all of my surroundings, describing them for Jane. I saw the sunflowers blooming on the windowsill and my teacher explaining the letters of the alphabet to the class. I remembered that I hated the sound of the chalk on the board and I immediately winced as an adult. The tables and chairs barely came up to my knee and I felt like a giant in this tiny room. At the back of the room, I saw little Jude trying to remain in his seat.

I saw myself stand up and the teacher immediately told me to sit down. I couldn't explain to her that the noise of the chalkboard was upsetting me and was the trigger for my latest outburst. Watching this, I felt the pain of my inner child, as the teacher couldn't hear my adult roars to stop writing on the chalkboard either. My classmates were staring at my younger self as I stood with my hands over my ears, refusing to sit down. I asked Jane if I could leave the scene and she declined, telling me I could take action instead.

I could see my face clearly, since Mum always had my school photos on display in our house. My school picture from that year sat above our television for almost twenty years. As I stared at myself as a child, I knew I had to do something. Eventually, my teacher realized the cause of my sorrow, and little Jude sat down.

I walked among the tiny tables and chairs to where I was sitting. I was still invisible to all concerned, except for me as a child. My childlike eyes locked on my towering adult frame as I approached. I knelt down beside him, held out my arms, and embraced him with the tightest hug that I could possibly give. I placed my hand on his thick black hair and I wanted to hold him forever.

While still kneeling, I looked upon myself as a child when our embrace ended. I looked him in the eye and gave my most heartfelt of apologies for resenting him for so long. I was just a child, the picture of innocence who obviously had struggles that nobody could understand. It wasn't his fault, nor was it anyone else's. As I stood up, I stopped feeling ashamed of him and myself. I finally let go and accepted my childhood for what it was; I could now make the steps toward healing. I looked down at myself as a child, and waved goodbye.

I imagined myself walking out of that classroom and closing the door, all while telling Jane everything that had happened. I walked down the corridor with a smile, as I knew I had finally confronted the demon that had restricted me for so long. I left the school and as I walked away I never looked back.

CHAPTER 12

W hen I finished my therapy, Ethan and I decided to go on holiday. We couldn't wait to escape to the sunshine for a week, and we both needed it. It was a family affair with my parents and Emily's family coming along, too. It had been a tough year so we all looked forward to it.

Ethan was incredibly excited and made it his mission to see how long he could remain in the swimming pool. I suffered the icy waters to have fun with him and he still talks about this holiday eighteen months later. I made a huge step in coming to terms with being different and I felt I had improved greatly.

We went to the beach and I lay on a sun lounger while Ethan built sand castles in front of me. He wanted to take off his sandals and I was hesitant at first. I remembered my therapy sessions, though, and decided to let him. I looked down at my own shoes and felt determined. Was I brave enough to overcome sand also? I unlaced my shoes, took off my ankle socks, and let my bare foot rest on the lounger. I contemplated the sand for a few seconds and then went for it! As soon as my bare foot touched the sand, my skin crawled and I quickly put my shoes back on.

Although I had completed my therapy and was building a better relationship with Ethan, there were some things that simply couldn't change. I still very much have Asperger's, and there are quirks that I know I will never be free of, including my discomfort with walking on strange surfaces.

I have always been naturally talented at problem solving, although I guess my biggest issue is also creating problems. As I now think somewhat differently because of the therapies, my brain is much slower and less active than it used to be, although it can still wreak havoc from time to time. Given my historic detachment from everyone and my clear vulnerability as a child, I still find it very difficult to trust people. This has affected me most in my romantic life, although I'm still very much a work in progress.

I am much more independent than I used to be and I've found my own way, at my own pace, in my own time. I couldn't have done it without all the educational and therapeutic support I received over the years. I'm eternally grateful for everyone who has taught me lessons in life, both positive and negative. I am much more resilient now and I'm in control of creating and living a happy life—and that includes providing Ethan with happiness.

Ethan started primary school in September 2018. He was so happy to have his own uniform and that he would meet lots of new friends. His mum and I took him to school for his first day and we got pictures with him in his uniform—I was so proud. He attends a different school than the one I went to, but it has similarities. I saw the tiny red chairs and low tables and it reminded me of my own primary school days. He has his own coat peg just like I had and there's even a picture of a car on his peg. Like father, like son!

Ethan is managing very well at school and loves going. He wears his school bag and uniform with pride when I leave him at school. It's nice to see him mix with his classmates, something I never could do. Ethan loves to talk about his day and we often still read books together.

He enjoys stories and learning to read them on his own. He always has to tell me to slow down because I read too fast.

I did end up leaving my job for a position closer to home. It was very hard leaving my previous team, although I knew I had to be closer to home for Ethan's sake. By now, everyone on the team knew that I had Asperger's and they were all accepting and understanding. I guess they knew to always take me with a grain of salt, and I still keep in touch with them today. It's nice being at home sooner in the evenings and having the chance to take Ethan to school in the morning, something I couldn't do if I still had a thirty-mile commute.

In the job I am in now, I told everyone that I had Asperger's from the start and they all understood. I wanted to start my new job on a foundation of honesty and to ensure I was entirely myself. It hasn't changed how anyone has viewed me or worked with me, although it made me feel better being honest with everyone from the start. Obviously, I should have done this many years ago, but my internal issues didn't allow me to. It was incredibly difficult.

I still enjoy planning my days and having my lists ready for the working day. My way of working certainly hasn't changed and I can still become annoyed if sudden changes occur that interfere with the day I have planned. My teammates tolerate my quirks with the utmost professionalism and it satisfies me to know that they understand me and accept me, despite all of my complexities.

Since I have opened up to everyone in my life about having Asperger's, I couldn't help but carry out more research. I often ignored all autism-related literature and refused to read anything about it. I have since joined various support groups on social media and I have found them very useful. Social media has connected people more than ever before and it can offer some safe places to talk.

I have gained amazing advice and support, although some new acquaintances were not as fortunate as me. I am so lucky to have my mum and dad behind me every step of the way. Although I'm an adult, I still talk things over with them. I discuss and analyze every important life decision with them and take their advice much more seriously than I did before. I would be lost without them. They saw my potential whenever nobody else wanted to see it. Remember that I had severe challenges at school, to the point that I nearly went to a special needs school. If anyone reading has a child displaying the behaviors I did, do not fear, there is hope. Patience, love, and perseverance are all that is needed.

My closest friends all know my secret now. When I actually told them, nobody was judgmental or surprised. I am such an obvious case that everyone knew and treated me the same way they would treat anybody else. In my mind, I genuinely believed that nobody ever knew I had Asperger's and that I hid it impeccably. It seems this wasn't the case.

I thought I was able to mask who I was with surgical accuracy and it turns out I couldn't. My work colleagues and friends always had their suspicions, but were obviously much too polite to mention them. Or if they did, I certainly didn't pick up on it. I still struggle with some cues and sometimes I need things spelled out to me—I haven't mastered subtlety just yet.

My attitude toward my childhood changed with the help of therapy. I couldn't have gotten to where I am now without it and if anyone is offered these supports, accept them with open arms. Pride is incredibly difficult to swallow, but despair and regret are much more difficult. Being a young man, I wanted to feel invincible, like I perceived every other man my age to be. Had I refused therapy, I don't know where I would be today. It was the hardest decision I ever made, but also the best one for Ethan and me.

The same message applies to medications. When I was in a good place, I made the mistake of refusing to take my medication and I paid the price. When I stopped my daily regimen, my symptoms came back full force and I fell so low that I didn't realize I needed them again. For me, the medication does work. Yes, I did feel quite lethargic and deflated for the first month, but I eventually improved. I have a better sleeping pattern and I don't find myself obsessing and worrying as much as I did. My advice is to stick with it.

Every weekend Ethan decides the running order of our days. I have delegated that duty to him and he has accepted it with his usual childlike excitement. Knowing that Ethan decides our weekend activity has become part of my routine and I can cope with this now. It actually relieves some of the pressure of having to entertain him and he always has good suggestions, although he can be disappointed when I tell him we can't go to the moon!

Ethan always greets me with a hug and a smile when I pick him up, and he loves spending time with me. Likewise, I love spending time with him. We go on adventures, play games, and watch films with our favorite snacks. He no longer lives in my shadow and I can only thank my therapists for helping me to realize that he was living in my shadow for those early years. He now draws pictures of me and he knows I have a love of the universe and interstellar space, so he often draws me with the moon and stars beside my bearded stick figure.

My story isn't a "happily ever after" type story. Although my life has improved, it has not been magically fixed. I still have my struggles and I often turn to my mum and dad for support like I always have. Emily has also played a major part in my success and was a listening ear when Mum and Dad were too tired to listen to me any further. I am very cynical by nature and I find it hard to trust. I'm sure this has cost me opportunities but I will learn one day.

Such was my vulnerability; I still find it difficult to forge meaningful relationships. I'm still not great at deciphering facial expressions and social cues, although I am learning to try. I now ask people to clarify what they mean or to explain things in a different way. While it takes some getting used to for others, it helps me better interact with them.

One evening, when searching the cupboards under my stairs, I found an old box. I couldn't remember what it contained or why it was in there, so I took everything out of the cupboard. I stood the Christmas tree, decorations, and old crockery aside to lift the mystery box. I took it into the living room, opened the box, and found it was full of old notebooks.

After lighting my fire and sitting in my armchair, I started looking through my old notebooks to see what they contained. Some were old notes I had written while waiting for Ethan to be born and others contained running diaries. I normally burned my notebooks so my parents wouldn't discover them, although many still survived. I couldn't believe the content. Pages filled with my fears before Ethan was born, and none of it transpired in the real world.

My incessant note-taking has always been one of my quirks. I have reduced it greatly in the past two years, although I'm not ready to let go of it just yet. My notepads and pens sit by my bedside and they comfort me knowing they are there. Reading my notes helps me visualize much more clearly; I can't take a mental note of anything. I even kept notes of Ethan's early days. In that moment by the fire, I closed my eyes and imagined Ethan as a baby sleeping in a basket beside my bed. Instead of watching my beautiful baby sleep and marveling at the wonder of life, I had instead wrote and wrote and wrote.

I placed the notebooks I had read beside the sofa in a neat pile and I heard the creak of the upstairs floorboards. Ethan came halfway down the stairs and peeked through the spindles of the staircase facing the living room door. He asked me what I was doing and he came into the living room, sat on the floor, and picked up my some of my notebooks. He asked if they were bedtime stories and if I could read him one. I read about his first few nights in my bedroom at my parent's house and he loved asking what our first room was like. Ethan quickly became bored when my notepads didn't contain astronauts or cowboys, so he went back to bed.

I was about to put the diaries back in the box when I saw one lurking at the bottom of the box. It looked awfully familiar and when I opened it, I realized it was my therapy diary. All the tasks and exercises were contained within it and I loved reading over it all again. I knew I hadn't wanted to throw my notepads away, but somehow I'd forgotten that I'd kept them.

As my fire crackled I had a thought. I laid all the notepads out in front of me and put them in chronological order. Some notepads didn't survive being burned those many years ago so some gaps existed in the timeline. I read them all again and I was overwhelmed at how far I had come. It was only six and a half years ago that my obsessions could have condemned me to a lifetime of misery. When I finished my therapy I didn't think much of it afterward until now.

I looked at the final exercise again and my perception toward my childhood. For years I resented myself as a child and placed him in the darkest dungeon of my memories. I was ashamed of him, so I kept him in the darkness and couldn't risk anyone seeing him. I had placed him so far away that I forgot about him as he screamed for his freedom. I couldn't allow this so I ignored the cries unconsciously and it was only after I set him free that I truly became happy.

After discovering all of my old notepads that night, I decided to write my story for Ethan and this book is it. I collected all the notebooks that would eventually become this story and after I finished the first draft of the manuscript, the notebooks were all burned like many before them.

In time I want Ethan to know who his dad is and what I went through. I told him I was writing a story about us and he asked if there would be any spaceships in it. I told him there would be, and by writing this paragraph I didn't break that promise!

Mum and Dad moved out of our family home and downsized to an apartment. I went inside our old family home when it was empty, and I could still feel the tension in my bedroom. I had sat for many hours in that house, descending into madness and dragging everyone I loved with me. I had so many happy memories growing up there, although I was happy to leave the dark memories behind when I closed the door and left for the final time.

Mum and Dad's new apartment building has a mostly vacant multi-story car park that Ethan loves to play in. Due to the car park being sheltered, he can ride his bike in the rain and burn some excess energy while he waits for me to return home from work. When I went to pick Ethan up yesterday, he challenged me to a race across the car park. Given my competitive nature I accepted, and I took my place at the starting line beside Ethan. With a roar, Ethan started the race and I jogged lightly behind him. Ethan was sprinting with all his strength to reach the other side before me. As I saw Ethan slowing down and struggling for breath, I caught up with him and without a second thought, I ran ahead of him. As we raced across the car park, I left Ethan in my dust and sprinted across the finish line. This is the most important lesson that I want to teach Ethan and everyone else.

Defeat makes a champion!

ERIN GROVER

Jude Morrow presented with communication and social difficulties early in life, which led to a diagnosis of Asperger Type Autism at the age of eleven. Despite having educational challenges, Jude progressed through secondary school and graduated from the University of Ulster with an Honors Degree in Social Work in 2012. Jude now works as a social worker and is a motivational speaker and advocate for all things autism. When not speaking, writing, or social working, Jude loves spending time with his son, Ethan, enjoying the outdoors, cooking, and reading.

Learn more about Jude's speaking tours, blog, and follow him on social media at www.judemorrow.com.